Essays in Economics and Other Cheerful Themes

Essays in Economics and Other Cheerful Themes

A Dismal Scientist's Occasional Reflections
on the World around Him

S. Subramanian

⑤SAGE www.sagepublications.com
Los Angeles • London • New Delhi • Singapore • Washington DC

First published in 2014 by

 SAGE Publications India Pvt Ltd
B1/I-1 Mohan Cooperative Industrial Area
Mathura Road, New Delhi 110 044, India
www.sagepub.in

SAGE Publications Inc
2455 Teller Road
Thousand Oaks, California 91320, USA

SAGE Publications Ltd
1 Oliver's Yard, 55 City Road
London EC1Y 1SP, United Kingdom

SAGE Publications Asia-Pacific Pte Ltd
3 Church Street
#10-04 Samsung Hub
Singapore 049483

Published by Vivek Mehra for SAGE Publications India Pvt Ltd, typeset in Bembo 11/13.7pt by Diligent Typesetter, Delhi and printed at Sai Print-O-Pack Pvt Ltd, New Delhi.

Library of Congress Cataloging-in-Publication Data Available

ISBN: 978-81-321-1373-7 (HB)

The SAGE Team: N. Unni Nair, Saima Ghaffar, Nand Kumar Jha and Dally Verghese

Shall we make a tale, boys, that things are sure to mend,
Playing bluff and hale, boys, waiting for the end?

William Empson

Thank you for choosing a SAGE product! If you have any comment,
observation or feedback, I would like to personally hear from you.
Please write to me at contactceo@sagepub.in

—Vivek Mehra, Managing Director and CEO,
SAGE Publications India Pvt. Ltd, New Delhi

Bulk Sales

SAGE India offers special discounts for purchase of books in bulk.
We also make available special imprints and excerpts from our
books on demand.

For orders and enquiries, write to us at

Marketing Department
SAGE Publications India Pvt. Ltd
B1/I-1, Mohan Cooperative Industrial Area
Mathura Road, Post Bag 7
New Delhi 110044, India
E-mail us at marketing@sagepub.in

Get to know more about SAGE, be invited to SAGE events, get on
our mailing list. Write today to marketing@sagepub.in

This book is also available as an e-book.

Contents

List of Tables

Preface

Academic scribblers (as J.M. Keynes called these children of misfortune), in their less academic moments, tend nevertheless to continue to be scribblers. For over thirty years now I have been writing pointless professional papers, with impossible titles such as 'Poverty Measures as Normalized Distance Functions' and 'Inequality Measurement with Subgroup Decomposability and Level Sensitivity', and this is the sort of thing, as I believe readers will readily appreciate, that can lead to depressive melancholia or worse (at the dispensing, no less than at the receiving, end of these effusions). The scribbler needs something to relieve the mindless tedium of her/his scribbling, and so ends up with some more—albeit less pronouncedly academic—scribbling. Therein lies the explanation and justification for, and defence of, this book. It is a product of the occasional busman's holiday I have resorted to over the years, and has resulted in the collection of a small number of my relatively less academic writings (both published and unpublished) in this volume, which I hope will prove to be of some interest to students of economy and society who haven't yet become full-time, formally ordained, and properly certified scholars.

The first part of the book (*Of Home and the World*) comprises three parts, titled, respectively, 'Global Deprivation and Disparity', 'Domestic Deprivation and Disparity', and 'Polity and Society'. This is a collection of nine essays that could be said to fall within the domain of concern of a development economist of a certain persuasion, which is perhaps best characterized as being old-fashioned and unrefined. The essays address the themes, directly or by allusion, of global and national justice; the obligations of a state to its citizens; the rights and well-being of the state's citizens;

poverty, inequality, and discrimination; social exclusion; and the arbitrary exercise of power by nations and peoples in possession of such power. Apart from the endemic problems of deprivation, disparity, and exclusion which have been so much a feature of India's development experience, specific events and issues—including the 2002 Gujarat pogrom and the debate on caste reservations—have been sought to be appraised.

The second part of the book (*Between Economics and Philosophy*) is perhaps analytically more demanding than the first part. It consists of four essays on themes at the intersection of economics, philosophy, and political science. The first essay is a brief consideration of the relative merits of the *proportion* and the *numbers* of people in poverty as the appropriate headcount indicator of deprivation. The second piece is an extended review of Amartya Sen's important book *The Idea of Justice*, and it is my hope that young readers of the essay will appreciate what an arid and indeed meaningless pursuit it can be to address issues of development policy that are not informed by normative values. A third essay seeks to rescue the credo of egalitarianism from a criticism directed at it by the moral philosopher Derek Parfit. Even social choice theory, which is generally considered to be a somewhat arcane aspect of economic theory, gets a look in, in the form of a popular account of a philosophical problem concerning the values of liberty and equality. (I may obtrude here the possibly useful information that for non-professionals and young scholars who have an interest in philosophical questions, two very useful sources of literature are the journal *Think: Philosophy for Everyone*, published for the Royal Institute of Philosophy, London, and the 'popular' magazine *Philosophy Now*.)

I am afraid there is also something in the volume on cricket, on film, on academic institutions and the affectations of their denizens, and on the convolutions of contemporary scholarly prose. These are collected in the third part of the book under the appropriately lowbrow heading of *Miscellaneous Mistakes*.

It is readily conceded that many of the essays collected here are weighed down by depressing themes: Thomas Carlyle would appear to have had a point when he described economics as a dismal science. The excuse for the persistent engagement with issues of deprivation and disparity must ultimately reside in the persistent presence of the phenomena of deprivation and disparity in our country. Here, George Mallory's reason for wishing to climb Everest is instructive ('because it's there'). It is worth noting though that poverty—unlike Mount Everest—ought *not* to be there: it is a rotten moral shame.

Often enough, the essays do not say anything notably novel or original, but what is even more remarkable is that the processes and outcomes which the essays describe continue, despite decades of the development experience, to remain so stalely and un-originally a feature of the surrounding social and economic landscape. Many of the essays also repeat themselves, despite my efforts at editing out the repetitions: I apologize for this and crave the reader's understanding by pointing out that the essays were written at different times for different audiences. I do not, however, apologize overmuch, because it is also arguable that repeating the same mundane truths over and over again, obstinately and stolidly, has something to commend it when the factors inspiring the truths have themselves yielded to such little, or no, mutation over the years.

This book is principally intended for young students of economics—undergraduates and postgraduates who are still not so 'mature' as to have quite forsaken their taste for reasoning and relevance in favour of the more alluring temptations of comfort and accommodation. If that sounds pompous—as no doubt it does—the putative young reader of this work is also invited to take a look at the penultimate essay in the volume, in which the author administers a well-deserved kick to his own hindquarters.

S. Subramanian
April 2013

Acknowledgements

Most of the pieces appearing in this book have been published previously: of the seventeen pieces featured in the volume, all but four have appeared in print earlier, in one form or another. The original sources of these pieces are cited in detail in the appropriate chapters. In what follows, the publishers and editors of these previously published items are acknowledged.

Thanks are owed to the Editor Siddharth Varadarajan of *The Hindu* for permission to reproduce Chapter 1 from an article in two parts published in the newspaper in 2001, and to the Editor Rammanohar Reddy of *Economic and Political Weekly* for permission to reproduce Chapters 2, 5, 7, 9, and 11, which appeared in various issues of the journal in the years 2008, 2011, 2002, 2006/2007, and 2009, respectively. Parts of Chapters 4 and 8 appeared in *The Oxford Companion to Economics in India*, edited by Kaushik Basu and published by Oxford University Press, Delhi, in 2007: my thanks to the Editor and the Publisher of this book. My thanks also to the Publisher (Elsevier) and the Editor of *International Review of Economics and Finance*: a part of Chapter 8 appeared as a part of a book review published in a 2005 issue of this journal. Chapter 10 was originally published in 2005 as a 'One-Pager' in the United Nations Development Programme's series and included in the September 2009 publication the *IPC-IG Collection of One-Pagers* (Brasilia: Brazil): I am grateful to the International Policy Centre for Inclusive Growth (Brasilia) for permission to reproduce the piece. Chapter 12 first appeared in a 2011 issue of the *Journal of Philosophical Economics*, and thanks are owed to its Editor, Valentin Cojanu, for permission to reproduce the article here. Chapter 13 is a slightly revised version of an essay which was originally published in a 2011 issue of the journal *Think*: the article is here reproduced with the kind permission of the publisher (Cambridge University Press) and the Editor (Stephen Law) of the journal. I am indebted to the Editor, Robert Haswell Fiske, of *The Vocabula Review* for permission to reproduce part 4 of Chapter 14, which originally appeared in a 2009 issue of the *Review* under the title 'Bad Language: Post Modern Bull...', and for Chapter 16, which also appeared in the *Review*, in a 2010 issue. Chapter 17 was originally published in the Delhi School of Economics student journal *Eostre* in a 2013 issue and is reproduced here by kind permission of the journal's Editors.

Finally, I am indebted to my friend and colleague D. Jayaraj for the use of his ideas in Chapter 3, and more generally for the benefit of advice from and conversation with him over several years of collaborative effort. I would also like to acknowledge the very deft suggestions for improvement made by an anonymous reviewer of this manuscript: I hope and trust I have done some justice to their advice.

Introduction: A Brief Guide to the Book

In what follows, I provide a brief guide to the book in the form of a set of summaries of the various chapters.

Chapter 1: Well-being and the World Today

A simple guide to the aspects of (income as well as non-income) deprivations and disparities, as they obtain, on the global landscape. Outcomes—in terms of country-specific distributions of income, literacy, child mortality, and a composite index of 'capability failure'—are reviewed, as also the processes accompanying and leading up to these outcomes: colonialism, unfair international trade practices, unproductive spending on debt reparation and conflict, structural adjustment, and the vagaries and niggardliness of international aid.

Chapter 2: Global Poverty, Inequality, and Aid Flows: A Rough Guide to Some Simple Justice

How one measures poverty and inequality has implications for a variety of policy interventions relating to fair allocation in a variety of institutional settings. The distribution of international aid is an important case in point. This essay reasserts the importance of certain old-fashioned questions relating to international aid: what is the quantum of aid available in relation to the need for it? How may patterns of allocation, at both the dispensing and receiving ends of aid, be determined so as to take account of both poverty and international inequality in the distribution of incomes? Can some simple and plausible rules of allocation be devised? If so, what correspondence does reality bear to such rules? The questions are addressed with the aid of some simple analytics relating to optimal budgetary intervention in the alleviation of poverty. The ideas discussed are clarified by means of data employed in elementary empirical illustrations.

Chapter 3: The Status of the Child in India

A development economist's perspective on the regrettably backward status of children in India, with reference to such dimensions of deprivation as undernutrition, ill health, illiteracy, infant and child mortality, sex-selective foeticide, and child labour, and the seriously deficient record of the State in addressing these problems.

Chapter 4: Human Development and Human Rights

An assessment of post-independence India's record of development with reference to the categories of 'positive freedom', 'negative freedom', and 'discrimination'. The essay points to the disappointing performance of Indian society and the Indian State in securing for the country's citizens certain elementary capabilities and certain basic liberties, and a minimally fair distribution of such capabilities and liberties across groups of individuals obtained from a partitioning of the population by caste, gender, and sector of origin.

Chapter 5: 'Inclusive Development' and the Quintile Income Statistic

The rhetoric of 'inclusive development' tends often to be lost in vague generalities, when it is not altogether absent in various processes on the ground or in state policy that claims to be inspired by its demands. The present essay suggests that in at least one specific and restricted area of application—the intersection of poverty, inequality, and growth—it should be possible to capture some elementary aspect of inclusiveness by monitoring trends, set against targets, of the 'quintile income' statistic. This statistic, which was proposed in earlier work by Kaushik Basu, is a simple and useful aid to verifying the reach of inclusiveness in a specific dimension of development, a theme that is elaborated on in the essay.

Chapter 6: Reprisal without Rectitude

A brief essay written shortly after 9/11, and commenting on the unilateralism, hubris, and subjectivity informing the 'allied' attack on Afghanistan in the immediate wake of the events of 11 September 2001.

Chapter 7: Moral Catastrophes and Immoral Reasoning

This essay was written in the aftermath of the genocidal communal attacks unleashed in Gujarat in 2002. It deals with two widely practised traditions of moral reasoning known as 'deontology' and 'consequentialism', respectively, and argues that a great deal of such reasoning employed in the assessment of the Gujarat catastrophe has been an exercise in confused logic and self-serving obfuscation, deployed in order to rationalize disengagement (or worse) with the horrors of Gujarat.

Chapter 8: Looking Back and Ahead

An essay inspired by the defeat of the ruling coalition in the 2004 General Elections. The contention, widely held by the pink press, that this was a vote against bad politics and good economics, is challenged with the suggestion that the electorate had delivered a verdict against an economics which was as bad as the politics practiced by the incumbent coalition. The challenges of the time are discussed, and the modest hope is expressed that certain elementary steps required to secure a measure of egalitarian social development will be implemented. The extravagance of these hopes has, since, been ruthlessly exposed by the record of squandered opportunities that marks the performance of the dispensation that was voted into power in 2004, and then again in 2009.

Chapter 9: Examining the 'Creamy Layer' Principle

Once the validity of the 'creamy layer' principle is acknowledged in any one dimension of application, or as an axiomatically appealing principle of equality at an abstract level, it would be inconsistent to deny its validity in other spheres of application. It therefore becomes a matter of some importance to submit the appeal of this principle to critical scrutiny. This essay does just this and also addresses some subsequent critical views on the piece that were advanced by two other commentators.

Chapter 10: Headcount Poverty Comparisons

In assessing the prevalence of poverty, should we take account of the *proportion* of the population in poverty or the *numbers* of the population in poverty? This brief essay is an invitation to the reader to engage with some of the analytics and ethics underlying the question just posed. The article is a guide to the proposition that a social scientist is often confronted with the task of having to deal with apparently simple, but actually complicated, logical and moral problems.

Chapter 11: Thinking Through Justice

An extended review of Amartya Sen's magisterial work *The Idea of Justice*. This is especially addressed to younger scholars as a reminder of how and why economics is enriched when it is informed by philosophy.

Chapter 12: Are Egalitarians Really Vulnerable to the Levelling-down Objection and the Divided World Example?

This essay is a quick critique of one aspect of Derek Parfit's criticism of Egalitarianism in his larger consideration of the claims of, and distinction between, Prioritarianism and Egalitarianism. It reviews issues relating to the 'Levelling-Down Objection' and the 'Divided World Example'. More specifically, it is argued that the Levelling-Down Objection is a serious problem only for Pure Telic Egalitarianism, not for Pluralist Telic Egalitarianism; and that even in a Divided World, one can have an egalitarian justification for preferring an equal distribution of a smaller sum of well-being to an unequal distribution of a larger sum. By these means, it is contended that Parfit's claim of the vulnerability of Egalitarianism to the Levelling-Down Objection and the Divided World Example is not sustainable. This chapter is once more a pointer to younger scholars that there is much which the disciplines of economics and philosophy can gain from each other.

Chapter 13: Can We Possibly Subscribe to Both Liberty and Equality at One and the Same Time?

This essay is again somewhat in the spirit of Chapters 8 and 13 and invites the reader to make some forays into the formal territory of logical and ethical reasoning, with a view to uncovering certain complications in the apparently straightforward pursuit of the principles of equality and liberty. The author, in developing his argument, employs the conventions of a branch of knowledge called social choice theory, which lies at the intersection of economics, logic, philosophy, and political science. An attempt is made to lead the reader gently into the intricacies of formal choice theory, by resort to an illustration of the underlying principles involved that draws on the fiction of P.G. Wodehouse.

Chapter 14: A Curmudgeon's Complaints

Some ill-tempered grouses in a lighter—if far from entirely unserious—vein on various contemporary headaches in Indian society, including cricket, institutions of higher learning, schooling, and impenetrable post-modern prose.

Chapter 15: Jai Ho Jeeves! (An Advanced Sociological Analysis of *Slumdog Millionaire*)

In which Bertie Wooster deconstructs *Slumdog Millionaire* with Jeeves' help…

Chapter 16: Language and Representation or, More Modestly, Mathematical Economics and Poverty

A parody of the author's own professional craft—the writing of economics as a compound of gobbledygookery and the dishonest presentation of serious social and human problems as arcane logical ones.

Chapter 17: Writing Economics in Exactly 300 Words: Two Samples in the Tradition of J.B. Morton ('Beachcomber')

Evidence that when one is dealing with economics, it is after all not such a long distance from dismal to delirious...

A Final Note

A few of the essays carry unpleasant things such as equations and the like. These have generally been stowed away in footnotes or endnotes and can be safely ignored by the general reader, but are available to the more technically oriented reader if she/he should be interested in pursuing them.

PART I

Of Home and the World

Global Deprivation
and Disparity

1

Well-being and the World Today*

Outcomes

In order to be able to assert, with the poet Browning, that 'all's right with the world', one would have to take a narrowly restricted and selective view of the world. For, judged according to certain elementary indicators of deprivation, the general picture of the world that emerges is one of extreme misery in large parts of it and considerable comfort in small parts.

There are many different ways in which deprivation can be measured. I shall adopt a particularly simple approach to that problem here. Deprivation, for our purposes, will be summarized in an index called the Capability Failure Ratio (CFR, for short), a version of which has been jointly developed, elsewhere, by my colleague Manabi Majumdar and myself, and which is akin in spirit to Mahbub ul Haq's 'Human Deprivation Measure' and the UNDP's

* This essay appeared in two parts in the 8 and 9 February 2001 issues of *The Hindu*. It is based on the text of an invited paper ('Aspects of Global Deprivation and Disparity: A Child's Guide to Some Simple-Minded Arithmetic') presented at a conference on 'North–South Relationships in the World Economy in the 21st Century: Inequalities, Well-being, Opportunities', held at L'Aquila, Italy, over 6–10 September 2000, and organized by the University of Rome 'La Sapienza'. The conference paper has been published in F. Carlucci and F. Marzano (eds) (2003), *Poverty, Growth and Welfare in the World Economy in the 21st Century*. Bern: Peter Lang.

'Human Poverty Index'. The CFR is a straightforward average of the headcount ratios of deprivation in three dimensions of human achievement: those of knowledge; child survival; and a decent, income-related standard of living. These three headcount ratios are the adult illiteracy rate, the under-5 mortality rate, and an income-poverty ratio that is derived as follows. First, I postulate an international poverty line which I take to be one-half the global per capita gross domestic product (GDP), and I certify all those countries to be income poor which have a per capita GDP less than the poverty line. The income–poverty headcount ratio is then defined to be simply the proportion of a poor country's population that would have to be eliminated so that its average per capita GDP may rise to the poverty line: this would correspond to the 'man overboard' solution to the familiar 'Life-Boat Ethics Dilemma'. (For a non-poor country, the income–poverty ratio will be taken to be zero.)

I have computed the values of the CFR's components for a set of 174 countries, which together are taken to constitute the 'world'. (These are the countries for which the UNDP's annual human development report (HDR) furnishes information on their 'human development indices'). The estimates are for the year 1997. Data on adult illiteracy are available in the HDR for 1999. Cross-country data on under-5 mortality can be found in the UNICEF's annual publication State of the World's Children, 1999. To calculate the country-wise income–headcount ratios of poverty, resort has been had to country-wise data on per capita GDP, measured in 'purchasing power parity (PPP)' dollars, again available in HDR, 1999. What do the numbers suggest?

The first component of the CFR is the adult illiteracy rate, whose global average value, at around 21 per cent, is less than flattering. This poor average performance is compounded by large dispersions around the mean: the adult illiteracy rate is as low as 1 per cent in 30 countries and in excess of 50 per cent in 26 countries. Grouped data bring out the contrasts more starkly, with figures, for Sub-Saharan Africa and the Arab states, of nearly 42 per cent; 28 per cent for Asia and the Pacific; nearly 13 per cent for Latin America and the Caribbean; and just 1.3 per cent for the industrialized countries.

The second component of the CFR is the under-5 mortality rate, which is widely known to be a crucial indicator of the socio-economic well-being of any society. The global average child mortality rate is 85 per 1,000 live births, which is less than an impressive record of achievement, unless one is content with the performance of countries such as Kenya and Gambia, each of which has a mortality rate of 87 per 1,000 live births. The average conceals wide inter-country differences, ranging from a child-mortality rate of 4 per 1,000 live births in the Scandinavian countries to a shocking rate of 320 for Niger and 316 for Sierra Leone. Indeed, sub-Saharan Africa as a whole, with a figure of 169 child deaths per 1,000 live births, exceeds the figure for its nearest 'competitor', Asia and the Pacific, by a factor of 200 per cent; and that for the industrialized countries, by a factor of 2,500 per cent. Such disparities are clearly seriously gross.

The third component of the CFR is the income-headcount measure of poverty, whose derivation has been explained earlier. The global average per capita GDP is PPP\$ 6,300; I shall pitch the international poverty line at PPP\$ 3,000, which is less than one-half of the world's mean. On this basis, it turns out that 68 countries, accounting for 39 per cent of the world's countries, are poor. The poverty headcount ratios for these countries range from 0.33 per cent for Cape Verde to a staggering 86.33 per cent for Sierra Leone. The polarities become apparent from a consideration of grouped data. Sub-Saharan Africa has an income–poverty ratio in excess of 60 per cent; Asia and the Pacific follow with 21 per cent; the Arab states and the Eastern Europe and Commonwealth of Independent states have figures of 10.1 and 8.2 per cent, respectively; and the industrialized countries have not a single poor country in their lot. Taking the world as a whole, the income–headcount ratio of poverty is high, at 18.6 per cent. The implication (making use of world population figures) is quite simply this: that every country would have an opportunity of escaping poverty if only 1,070 million people in the poorest countries (adding up to more than 127 per cent of the combined population of all the industrialized countries) would just obligingly cease to exist.

Finally, I aggregate the components of the CFR in order to present a consolidated picture of capability failure in the dimensions of knowledge, child survival, and income. The numbers suggest the immense handicap under which Sub-Saharan Africa labours: its CFR is nearly 40 per cent, which is around twice as high as the figures for two other very badly performing groups of countries, namely the Arab states and the Asia and Pacific countries. By contrast, the CFR for the industrialized countries group is less than 1 per cent. For the world as a whole, the CFR is in excess of 16 per cent. The picture in a nutshell: a high rate of global deprivation rendered significantly worse by its highly unequal distribution across countries.

While on the subject of deprivation and disparity, it is instructive to take a closer look at global poverty and inequality in the dimension of income. As we have already seen, there is a great deal of income poverty in the world today. What can one say of the international burden of poverty, that is, of the relative difficulty or otherwise of alleviating poverty through redistributive effort? It would appear that the burden of poverty is very small in relation to the magnitude of poverty itself. Illustrative of this is the fact that the aggregate shortfall from the income needed to escape poverty, for the set of 68 poor countries I have alluded to earlier, is only around 16 per cent of the combined GDP of the Southern European and industrialized groups of countries (the only groups without a single poor nation in their lot). This is a testimony to the very large 'slack' available in the world, and which arises from the considerable levels of global inequality it accommodates.

Indeed, it turns out that the statistical measure of dispersion called the Gini coefficient assumes a high value of 0.55 when computed for the cross-country distribution of incomes in PPP dollars. To comprehend what this implies in terms that are easily understood, one can make use of an equivalence result that asserts that a Gini value of G for any n-person distribution is equivalent to a share of $(1-G)/2$ going to the poorer of two persons in a two-person cake-sharing problem. A global Gini of 0.55 can then be interpreted in the following terms. It is 'as if there were two entities—call them 'North' and 'South'—such that South receives a little less than 23 per cent of the world's income cake, with North appropriating the remaining 77 per cent. This is the rather stark picture of polarization to which the actual picture of global income inequality that obtains can be equivalently reduced.

There are many ways of measuring income inequality, and while I do not report on the results here, all the measures are united in revealing large levels of global income disparity. Nearly 30 years ago Amartya Sen wrote a book called *On Economic Inequality*, which he dedicated to his daughters 'with the expectation that when they grow up they will find less of it no matter how they decide to measure it'. But today, no matter how one measures global inequality, one ends up, again and again, finding a great deal too much of it. What makes it worse is that, by all accounts, there has been more and more of it to be found over time, as a perusal of the UNDP's HDR over the decade of the 90s will testify.

Processes

In the first part of this two-part article, I dealt with certain findings, relating to aspects of global deprivation and disparity, in the space of outcomes. In this the second part, I consider certain processes, from a global perspective, that must be considered to be salient factors in any explanation of the unhappy outcomes reviewed earlier.

A first major phenomenon demanding attention is that of colonialism. It is no accident that of the 68 poor countries that were identified in Part I of this article, as many as 54 (making for a proportion of 79 per cent) have had an earlier history of colonial rule; and the average age from independence of these 54 countries is just over 51 years. These facts should serve to guard against juvenile celebrations of Henry Ford's profundity regarding history being bunk.

A second major issue of relevance is that of international trade. Professor T.N. Srinivasan has written a richly informative monograph (*Developing Countries and the Multilateral Trading System: From GATT to the Uruguay Round and the Future*; Oxford University Press, New Delhi, 1998) which is a vital sourcebook on the subject. The evidence he has reviewed on the history of the first seven rounds of multilateral trade negotiations (MTNs) presided over by the General Agreement on Tariffs and Trade (GATT), from Havana 1947 to Tokyo 1979, is compatible with an interpretation which he provides—one which, I suspect, many of his readers will find wholly convincing, though the author himself, strangely, appears to have difficulty in wholeheartedly accepting it—namely, that 'in sum, the GATT was unfriendly, if not actively hostile, to the interests of developing countries'. The eighth, or Uruguay, round of MTNs, which commenced at Puenta del Este in 1986 and wound its tortuous way to Marrakesh (Morocco) in 1994, and paved the way for the birth of the World Trade Organization (WTO) in 1995, marked a new and particularly aggressive assertion of developed country interests. John Croome has provided a comprehensive account of the eighth round in his book *Reshaping the World Trading System: A History of the Uruguay Round* (WTO, Geneva, 1995). In the matter of market access; of liberalization of trade in natural resource and tropical products; of bringing agriculture within the discipline of GATT; of the pace governing the dissolution of the GATT-inconsistent bilateral arrangements governing trade in textiles and clothing; of the import of trade-related intellectual property rights, trade-related investment measures and trade in services within the ambit of negotiations; of securing safeguards against unfair trade practices such as anti-dumping measures; of facilitating the impartial prosecution of dispute-settlement; of linking trade to environmental and labour standards: in all of these matters, it would be fair to suggest that the balance of advantage has been disproportionately weighted in favour of the developed countries and against the developing ones. In an overall appraisal of the role of international trade in the division of global advantage, one is compelled to the conclusion that while power will continue to work for the North, the rules have begun to work against the South.

A third issue of consequence is the international debt burden borne by developing countries. By any reckoning, a country should be seen to be in a poorly debt-sustainable situation if the ratio of the present value of debt to the export of goods and services is in excess of 200 per cent. World Bank data for 1996 suggest that there are 42 countries in this state of indebtedness, of which, significantly, 25 belong to Sub-Saharan Africa. Further, one finds that 28 of the 42 most deprived countries, in terms of the CFR reviewed earlier, figure also in the list of 42 heavily indebted countries. While the debt burden of poor countries is a major brake on their development, it is instructive to ask what sort of burden a write-off of these debts would constitute for the richer nations. To get things in perspective, consider the set of acutely poor nations, defined as those with a per capita GDP which is less than PPP$ 1,500 (which is a quarter of the global average per capita GDP). There are 35 countries in this league. For 34 of these countries taken together, and on which data in HDR (1999) are available, it turns out that the combined ratio, in 1997, of external debt (ED) to gross national product (GNP) is cripplingly high, at 82.3 per cent. But the ED of these same countries taken together, as a proportion of the combined GNP of 17 of the richest countries of the world, is a piffling 0.7 per cent. The substantive question 'Am I my brother's keeper?' must find an answer which is located outside of the province of simple sums.

Of material relevance is the fourth issue of military spending. HDR (1999) data suggest that, in terms of 1993–97 totals, the 10 major conventional weapons exporting countries were among the ones with the lowest CFRs, whereas the 10 major importing countries were among those with high rates of capability failure. It would appear that countries that can ill-afford to spend money on guns are buying them in a big way, whereas those countries that are among the best-placed ones are doing the bulk of the selling. The combined burden of debt-servicing and military expenditure, and the way in which public spending in these unproductive areas crowds out desperately needed resources for social sector spending, becomes clear from a reading of selected data distributed through the HDR, 1999. Here is information on the ratio of per capita spending on debt-servicing and military-related matters to per capita spending on education and health, in 1997, for a sample of six developing countries; India: 125 per cent; Croatia: 141 per cent; Uganda: 159 per cent; Pakistan: 285 per cent; Nigeria: 370 per cent; and Indonesia: 453 per cent. Debt and strife are an effective recipe for keeping knowledge and good health out of the reach of a country's citizens.

To the issues reviewed above must be added a fifth important one: that of 'adjustment'. From towards the end of the 1970s, and into the 1980s and the 1990s, a number of Sub-Saharan African, Latin American and Caribbean, and Asian countries faced unprecedentedly harsh economic crises arising from a variety of causes. The twin, Bank-Fund remedies for these crises were a standard package of macroeconomic stabilization and structural adjustment. The aim of the first measure is to correct macroeconomic imbalances by dampening demand, and to set the scene for structural adjustment policies to work out the longer-term 'reform' outcomes of efficient resource allocation, liberalization, recovery, and growth. Giovanni Cornia and Frances Stewart, in their work on 'Country Experience with Adjustment' (1987), suggest that in 6 of the 10 countries studied by them in the 80s, macro-balance was secured at the cost of welfare in three countries, welfare was secured at the cost of macro-balance in one country, and both suffered in two countries. Stewart's (1994) subsequent work on adjustment and its impact on education ('Education and Adjustment: The Experience of the 1980s and Lessons for the 1990s') reveals that in a number of African and Latin American countries undergoing structural adjustment in the 1980s, education was adversely affected, in terms of both supply and demand side effects. Given the instrumental importance of education for other forms of human well-being, the costs of a certain sort of 'reform' must be judged to be very steep indeed.

This brings us to our sixth issue: might not international aid be the solution to all these problems? As far back as 1969, a commission headed by Lester Pearson persuaded donor countries to commit 0.7 per cent of their GNP to aid. A look at the performance of the 21 member countries of the OECD's development assistance committee suggests that, with the exception of the Nordic countries, the 0.7 per cent recommendation has been observed only in the breach. Calculations based on data from HDR (1999) suggest that if the entire overseas development assistance received by different groups of countries in 1997 were to be made exclusively available to the 68 income-poor countries of the world, then the average annual aid received by a member of this group of countries would work out to US\$ 18.27 per year, or a dollar 52 cents per month, or (assuming 30 days to a month and resorting to more sordid division) to 5 cents a day.

The above review of outcomes and processes suggests that a developing country is best advised, despite all its debilities, to look to itself and other similarly placed countries, in order to overcome its deprivations. For one thing, there is, judging from the evidence, little realistic prospect of the North coming to the aid of the South; and there is much to be said for South–South cooperation. For another, the opportunities that reside in the unfulfilled potential of fair, reasonably egalitarian and democratic internal governance need urgently to be exploited. In the specific context of India, I should like to submit that the means to realizing the promise of what Amartya Sen has called development as freedom does not reside in lynching missionaries and demolishing mosques.

References

Cornia, G. A. and F. Stewart. (1987), 'Country Experience with Adjustment', in G. A. Cornia, R. Jolly and F. Stewart (eds.) *Adjustment with a Human Face, Volume 2, Ten Country Case Studies*. Clarendon Press: Oxford.

Stewart, F. (1994), 'Education and Adjustment: The Experience of the 1980s and Lessons for the 1990s', in R. Prendergast and F. Stewart (eds.) *Market Forces and World Development*. Macmillan: Basingstoke.

2

Global Poverty, Inequality, and Aid Flows: A Rough Guide to Some Simple Justice*

Introduction

This is an old-fashioned essay that will re-assert some old-fash-ioned views on international aid, global poverty, and inter-country inequality. The literature on aid allocation has become increasingly complex, nuanced, and fine-tuned, but often at the cost of disengagement with certain large and undeniable truths which are crucially germane to the issue. The present essay attempts to keep the broader picture in view while dealing with some simple rules of aid allocation which are motivated by considerations of 'how much?', 'from whom?', and 'to whom?'. In the process, it addresses the following questions. How much poverty is there in the world? How much aid is available in relation to the need for it? How onerous is the redistributive effort entailed in eradicating global poverty? What relation do the amounts of aid disbursed by

*This article was originally published as: 'Global Poverty, Inequality, and Aid Flows: A Rough Guide to Some Simple Justice' (2008): *Economic and Political Weekly*, 43(46): 53–63.

different countries have to the relative capabilities of these donor countries? What relation does the pattern of aid receipt bear to the relative needs of beneficiary countries? These issues are addressed largely within the framework of a simple analysis of optimal budgetary intervention in the redress of poverty.

It should be emphasized that the 'empirical' content of this essay is not distinguished by any particular care devoted to the complete reliability or 'up-to-dateness' of the data employed. The overall objective is no more than to present rough orders of magnitude of a set of indicators and statistics relevant to an assessment of the aid problem. This essay is based very considerably on Subramanian (2003) and especially on Subramanian (2007); and the idea is simply to convey an impressionistic picture—without being distracted by peripheral issues—of certain aspects of international aid in the context of global poverty and inequality. Insofar as it has proved possible, all formalisms have been relegated to footnotes which are likely to be of interest only to the specialist, and which therefore can be ignored by the non–specialist.

The Magnitude of Global Poverty

We use 2005 data on country-wise GDP, population, aid disbursement, and aid receipt from the UNDP's *HDR 2007–08*. *HDR 2007–08* presents information on a variety of socio-economic indicators for a set of 177 countries. Information on GDP, population, and aid receipt is available for a set of 174 countries which, together, we shall treat as constituting the 'world'. Before proceeding further it is as well to point out that all monetary aggregates in this paper are in terms of nominal US dollars, uncorrected for inter-country price differentials: while there may be a case for employing Purchasing Power Parity (PPP) exchange rates in order to present monetary aggregates in 'real' terms, this exercise has not been undertaken in the present paper. For one thing, the paper would become disproportionately bloated if all the relevant money-metric statistics were to be re-tabulated and re-interpreted in PPP-dollar terms. For another, the emphasis in this paper, as already stated, is on broad approaches, principles, magnitudes, trends, and tendencies, rather than on precision-claiming complications of detail.

The per capita GDP in 2005 for the set of 174 countries under consideration, at current prices, is 7,051 US dollars (see Table 2.1). It seems reasonable to suggest that a country should be deemed to be *poor* if its per capita GDP is less than 1,400 US dollars. Unquestionably, this is an arbitrary judgement, but arguably not an unreasonable one. An international poverty line which is pitched at less than a fifth of the global per capita GDP can scarcely attract the criticism of excessive liberalism, considering that the national poverty line in many advanced Western countries is set at one-half the median family income.

Table 2.1
Cross-Country Data on GDP, Population, and Aid Receipt, 2005

No.	Country	GDP (US$ billions)	Per capita GDP (US$)	Aid receipt (US$ millions)	Population (millions)
1	Luxembourg	36.5	79,851		0.4571
2	Norway	295.5	63,918		4.6231
3	Iceland	15.8	53,290		0.2965
4	Qatar	42.5	52,240		0.8136
5	Switzerland	367	49,351		7.4365
6	Ireland	201.8	48,524		4.1588
7	Denmark	258.7	47,769		5.4156
8	United States	12,416.50	41,890		296.4073
9	Sweden	357.7	39,637		9.0244
10	Netherlands	624.2	38,248		16.3198
11	Austria	306.1	37,175		8.2340
12	Finland	193.2	36,820		5.2471
13	United Kingdom	2,198.80	36,509		60.2262
14	Australia	732.5	36,032		20.3292
15	Japan	4,534.00	35,484		127.7759
16	Belgium	370.8	35,389		10.4778
17	France	2,126.60	34,936		60.8713

Table 2.1 continued

Table 2.1 continued

No.	Country	GDP (US$ billions)	Per capita GDP (US$)	Aid receipt (US$ millions)	Population (millions)
18	Canada	1,113.80	34,484		32.2990
19	Germany	2,794.90	33,890		82.4698
20	Kuwait	80.8	31,861		2.5360
21	Italy	1,762.50	30,073		58.6074
22	United Arab Emirates	129.7	28,612		4.5331
23	Singapore	116.8	26,893		4.3431
24	New Zealand	109.3	26,664		4.0992
25	Spain	1,124.60	25,914		43.3974
26	Hong Kong, China (SAR)	177.7	25,592		6.9436
27	Cyprus	15.4	20,841		0.7389
28	Greece	225.2	20,282		11.1034
29	Israel	123.4	17,828		6.9217
30	Bahrain	12.9	17,773		0.7258
31	Bahamas	5.5	17,497		0.3143
32	Portugal	183.3	17,376		10.5490
33	Slovenia	34.4	17,173		2.0031
34	Brunei Darussalam	6.4	17,121		0.3738
35	Korea (Republic of)	787.6	16,309		48.2924
36	Malta	5.6	13,803		0.4057
37	Saudi Arabia	309.8	13,399	26.3	23.1211
38	Czech Republic	124.4	12,152		10.2370
39	Barbados	3.1	11,465	–2.1	0.2704
40	Trinidad and Tobago	14.4	11,000	–2.1	1.3091
41	Hungary	109.2	10,830		10.0831
42	Antigua and Barbuda	0.9	10,578	7.2	0.0851
43	Estonia	13.1	9,733		1.3459
44	Oman	24.3	9,584	30.7	2.5355
45	Saint Kitts and Nevis	0.5	9,438	3.5	0.0530

Table 2.1 continued

Table 2.1 continued

No.	Country	GDP (US$ billions)	Per capita GDP (US$)	Aid receipt (US$ millions)	Population (millions)
46	Croatia	38.5	8,666	125.4	4.4426
47	Slovakia	46.4	8,616		5.3853
48	Seychelles	0.7	8,209	18.8	0.0853
49	Poland	303.2	7,945		38.1624
50	Lithuania	25.6	7,505		3.4111
51	Mexico	768.4	7,454	189.4	103.0856
52	Chile	115.2	7,073	151.7	16.2873
53	Latvia	15.8	6,879		2.2968
54	Libyan Arab Jamahiriya	38.8	6,621	24.4	5.8601
55	Equatorial Guinea	3.2	6,416	39	0.4988
56	Lebanon	21.9	6,135	243	3.5697
57	Botswana	10.3	5,846	70.9	1.7619
58	Gabon	8.1	5,821	53.9	1.3915
59	Russian Federation	763.7	5,336		143.1222
60	Venezuela (Bolivarian Republic of)	140.2	5,275	48.7	26.5782
61	Malaysia	130.3	5,142	31.6	25.3403
62	South Africa	239.5	5,109	700	46.8781
63	Mauritius	6.3	5,059	31.9	1.2453
64	Turkey	362.5	5,030	464	72.0676
65	Saint Lucia	0.8	5,007	11.1	0.1598
66	Uruguay	16.8	4,848	14.6	3.4653
67	Panama	15.5	4,786	19.5	3.2386
68	Argentina	183.2	4,728	99.7	38.7479
69	Costa Rica	20	4,627	29.5	4.3225
70	Romania	98.6	4,556		21.6418
71	Grenada	0.5	4,451	44.9	0.1123
72	Brazil	796.1	4,271	191.9	186.3966
73	Dominica	0.3	3,938	15.2	0.0762
74	Belize	1.1	3,786	12.9	0.2905
75	Kazakhstan	57.1	3,772	229.2	15.1379

Table 2.1 continued

Table 2.1 continued

No.	Country	GDP (US$ billions)	Per capita GDP (US$)	Aid receipt (US$ millions)	Population (millions)
76	Saint Vincent and the Grenadines	0.4	3,612	4.9	0.1107
77	Jamaica	9.6	3,607	35.7	2.6615
78	Bulgaria	26.6	3,443		7.7258
79	Dominican Republic	29.5	3,317	77	8.8936
80	Fiji	2.7	3,219	64	0.8388
81	Algeria	102.3	3,112	370.6	32.8728
82	Belarus	29.6	3,024	53.8	9.7884
83	Namibia	6.1	3,016	123.4	2.0225
84	Suriname	1.3	2,986	44	0.4354
85	Tunisia	28.7	2,860	376.5	10.0350
86	Peru	79.4	2,838	397.8	27.9774
87	Macedonia (TFYR)	5.8	2,835	230.3	2.0459
88	Iran (Islamic Republic of)	189.8	2,781	104	68.2488
89	Ecuador	36.5	2,758	209.5	13.2342
90	Thailand	176.6	2,750	–171.1	64.2182
91	Colombia	122.3	2,682	511.1	45.6003
92	Albania	8.4	2,678	318.7	3.1367
93	Bosnia and Herzegovina	9.9	2,546	546.1	3.8885
94	Guatemala	31.7	2,517	253.6	12.5944
95	El Salvador	17	2,467	199.4	6.8910
96	Swaziland	2.7	2,414	46	1.1185
97	Maldives	0.8	2,326	66.8	0.3439
98	Jordan	12.7	2,323	622	5.4671
99	Samoa	0.4	2,184	44	0.1832
100	Tonga	0.2	2,090	31.8	0.0957
101	Angola	32.8	2,058	441.8	15.9378
102	Cape Verde	1	1,940	160.6	0.5155
103	Ukraine	82.9	1,761	409.6	47.0755
104	China	2,234.30	1,713	1,756.90	1304.3199

Table 2.1 continued

Table 2.1 continued

No.	Country	GDP (US$ billions)	Per capita GDP (US$)	Aid receipt (US$ millions)	Population (millions)
105	Morocco	51.6	1,711	651.8	30.1578
106	Turkmenistan	8.1	1,669	28.3	4.8532
107	Armenia	4.9	1,625	193.3	3.0154
108	Azerbaijan	12.6	1,498	223.4	8.4112
109	Georgia	6.4	1,429	309.8	4.4787
110	Syrian Arab Republic	26.3	1,382	77.9	19.0304
111	Bhutan	0.8	1,325	90	0.6038
112	Indonesia	287.2	1,302	2,523.50	220.5837
113	Congo	5.1	1,273	1,448.90	4.0063
114	Paraguay	7.3	1,242	51.1	5.8776
115	Egypt	89.4	1,207	925.9	74.0679
116	Sri Lanka	23.5	1,196	1,189.30	19.6488
117	Philippines	99	1,192	561.8	83.0537
118	Honduras	8.3	1,151	680.8	7.2111
119	Occupied Palestinian Territories	4	1,107	1,101.60	3.6134
120	Guyana	0.8	1,048	136.8	0.7634
121	Cameroon	16.9	1,034	413.8	16.3443
122	Bolivia	9.3	1,017	582.9	9.1445
123	Nicaragua	4.9	954	740.1	5.1363
124	Côte d'Ivoire	16.3	900	119.1	18.1111
125	Djibouti	0.7	894	78.6	0.7830
126	Papua New Guinea	4.9	840	266.1	5.8333
127	Lesotho	1.5	808	68.8	1.8564
128	Sudan	27.5	760	1,828.60	36.1842
129	Nigeria	99	752	6,437.30	131.6489
130	Mongolia	1.9	736	211.9	2.5815
131	India	805.7	736	1,724.10	1094.7011
132	Yemen	15.1	718	335.9	21.0306
133	Pakistan	110.7	711	1,666.50	155.6962
134	Senegal	8.2	707	689.3	11.5983

Table 2.1 continued

Table 2.1 continued

No.	Country	GDP (US$ billions)	Per capita GDP (US$)	Aid receipt (US$ millions)	Population (millions)
135	Moldova	2.9	694	191.8	4.1787
136	Comoros	0.4	645	25.2	0.6202
137	Viet Nam	52.4	631	1,904.90	83.0428
138	Solomon Islands	0.3	624	198.2	0.4808
139	Zambia	7.3	623	945	11.7175
140	Mauritania	1.9	603	190.4	3.1509
141	Chad	5.5	561	379.8	9.8039
142	Kenya	18.7	547	768.3	34.1865
143	Uzbekistan	14	533	172.3	26.2664
144	Benin	4.3	508	349.1	8.4646
145	Haiti	4.3	500	515	8.6000
146	Lao People's Democratic Republic	2.9	485	295.7	5.9794
147	Ghana	10.7	485	1,119.90	22.0619
148	Kyrgyzstan	2.4	475	268.5	5.0526
149	Sao Tome and Principe	0.1	451	31.9	0.2217
150	Cambodia	6.2	440	537.8	14.0909
151	Bangladesh	60	423	1,320.50	141.8440
152	Mali	5.3	392	691.5	13.5204
153	Burkina Faso	5.2	391	659.6	13.2992
154	Timor-Leste	0.3	358	184.7	0.8380
155	Togo	2.2	358	86.7	6.1453
156	Tajikistan	2.3	355	241.4	6.4789
157	Guinea	3.3	350	182.1	9.4286
158	Central African Republic	1.4	339	95.3	4.1298
159	Mozambique	6.6	335	1,285.90	19.7015
160	Tanzania (United Republic of)	12.1	316	1,505.10	38.2911
161	Gambia	0.5	304	58.2	1.6447
162	Uganda	8.7	303	1,198.00	28.7129

Table 2.1 continued

Table 2.1 continued

No. Country	GDP (US$ billions)	Per capita GDP (US$)	Aid receipt (US$ millions)	Population (millions)
163 Nepal	7.4	272	427.9	27.2059
164 Madagascar	5	271	929.2	18.4502
165 Zimbabwe	3.4	259	367.7	13.1274
166 Niger	3.4	244	515.4	13.9344
167 Rwanda	2.2	238	576	9.2437
168 Eritrea	1	220	355.2	4.5455
169 Sierra Leone	1.2	216	343.4	5.5556
170 Guinea-Bissau	0.3	190	79.1	1.5789
171 Malawi	2.1	161	575.3	13.0435
172 Ethiopia	11.2	157	1,937.30	71.3376
173 Congo (Democratic Republic of the)	7.1	123	1,827.60	57.7236
174 Burundi	0.8	106	365	7.5472
Aggregate	44,043.5	7,050.999	59,584.6	6,246.42

Source: Tables 14 and 18 of *HDR 2007–08*. (Population figures have been obtained by dividing GDP figures by corresponding per capita GDP figures in Table 14 of *HDR 2007–08*.)

We shall, for the most part, not be concerned with the *intra-country* distribution of income: the assumption will be that within any country, each person receives its per capita income. (We shall, however, have occasion at a later stage to consider some relevant complications which arise from reckoning inequality in the intra-national distribution of income.) Each country can be described in terms of a pair of numbers, the first of which is its per capita GDP, and the second its population size. The global distribution of income can then be represented by a list of these pairs for all countries of the world. Table 2.2 presents information on the distribution of income for the poor countries of the world. One requires information on the global distribution of income and the poverty line in order to obtain an estimate of global poverty.[1]

A widely employed means of measuring poverty is in terms of a family of poverty indices advanced by Foster, Greer, and Thorbecke (1984). This is the so-called P_α family, where α is a parameter

Table 2.2
Distribution of Income in Poor Countries, 2005

No.	Country	Per capita GDP (US$)	Population (millions)
1	Syrian Arab Republic	1,382	19.0304
2	Bhutan	1,325	0.6038
3	Indonesia	1,302	220.5837
4	Congo	1,273	4.0063
5	Paraguay	1,242	5.8776
6	Egypt	1,207	74.0679
7	Sri Lanka	1,196	19.6488
8	Philippines	1,192	83.0537
9	Honduras	1,151	7.2111
10	Occupied Palestinian Territories	1,107	3.6134
11	Guyana	1,048	0.7634
12	Cameroon	1,034	16.3443
13	Bolivia	1,017	9.1445
14	Nicaragua	954	5.1363
15	Côte d'Ivoire	900	18.1111
16	Djibouti	894	0.7830
17	Papua New Guinea	840	5.8333
18	Lesotho	808	1.8564
19	Sudan	760	36.1842
20	Nigeria	752	131.6489
21	Mongolia	736	2.5815
22	India	736	1094.7011
23	Yemen	718	21.0306
24	Pakistan	711	155.6962
25	Senegal	707	11.5983
26	Moldova	694	4.1787
27	Comoros	645	0.6202
28	Viet Nam	631	83.0428
29	Solomon Islands	624	0.4808
30	Zambia	623	11.7175
31	Mauritania	603	3.1509

Table 2.2 continued

Table 2.2 continued

No.	Country	Per capita GDP (US$)	Population (millions)
32	Chad	561	9.8039
33	Kenya	547	34.1865
34	Uzbekistan	533	26.2664
35	Benin	508	8.4646
36	Haiti	500	8.6000
37	Lao People's Democratic Republic	485	5.9794
38	Ghana	485	22.0619
39	Kyrgyzstan	475	5.0526
40	Sao Tome and Principe	451	0.2217
41	Cambodia	440	14.0909
42	Bangladesh	423	141.8440
43	Mali	392	13.5204
44	Burkina Faso	391	13.2992
45	Timor–Leste	358	0.8380
46	Togo	358	6.1453
47	Tajikistan	355	6.4789
48	Guinea	350	9.4286
49	Central African Republic	339	4.1298
50	Mozambique	335	19.7015
51	Tanzania (United Republic of)	316	38.2911
52	Gambia	304	1.6447
53	Uganda	303	28.7129
54	Nepal	272	27.2059
55	Madagascar	271	18.4502
56	Zimbabwe	259	13.1274
57	Niger	244	13.9344
58	Rwanda	238	9.2437
59	Eritrea	220	4.5455
60	Sierra Leone	216	5.5556
61	Guinea-Bissau	190	1.5789
62	Malawi	161	13.0435

Table 2.2 continued

Table 2.2 continued

No.	Country	Per capita GDP (US$)	Population (millions)
63	Ethiopia	157	71.3376
64	Congo (Democratic Republic of the)	123	57.7236
65	Burundi	106	7.5472
	Aggregate	722.68	2,714.3564

Source: Table 14 of *HDR 2007–08*.
Note: A 'poor country' is one with a per capita GDP of less than 1,400 US$.

that assumes non-negative values and reflects a degree of 'aversion to poverty', with higher values of α signifying greater aversion to poverty.[2] As is well-known, P_0 is the *headcount ratio*, or proportion of the world's population living in its poor countries. The headcount ratio violates the *monotonicity axiom*, which is the requirement that, other things equal, a diminution in any poor person's income should increase poverty. This index also violates the *transfer axiom*, which is the requirement that, other things remaining the same, any equalizing redistribution of income among the poor should reduce poverty. For positive values of α strictly less than 1, P_α satisfies monotonicity but violates transfer: in fact, it favours *dis*-equalizing transfers among the poor. P_1 is the *per capita income-gap ratio*, or the proportionate deviation of the average income of the poor from the poverty line, expressed in per person terms; this index also satisfies monotonicity without satisfying transfer: it is sensitive only to the aggregate poverty gap and not to its interpersonal distribution. The index P_2, by contrast, does attend to distributional considerations: it satisfies both the monotonicity and the transfer axioms.[3] Using information on the global distribution of income (Table 2.2), the values of P_0, $P_{0.5}$, P_1, and P_2 can be computed. These turn out to be, respectively, 0.44, 0.29, 0.21, and 0.12. Familiarity with corresponding values of these indices for known poor countries suggests that the extent of global poverty is very considerable. This leads to our

First Observation: There is a lot of poverty in the world.

Aid in Relation to its Need

Let D_i stand for the ith *poorest country's deficit*, or total shortfall of income from what is required in order to escape poverty. The *aggregate global deficit* is D, which is obtained by summing the deficits of all the poor countries.[4] Table 2.3 provides information on the country-wise and total deficit for the set of poor countries. The aggregate deficit D is of the order of 1,838.5 billion US dollars. Data on aid disbursed by various countries, available in Table 17 of *HDR 2007–08*, suggest that the total quantum of aid disbursed in 2005 was of the order of 110 billion US dollars. The amount of aid available, as a proportion of aid required to eradicate global poverty, works out to 6 per cent. This leads to our

> *Second Observation: The quantum of aid available, in relation to the need for it, is vanishingly small.*

Table 2.3
Poverty Deficits of Poor Countries, 2005

No.	Country	Poverty line (US$)	Per capita GDP (US$)	Per capita deficit (poverty line-per capita GDP in US$)	Population (millions)	Total poverty deficit (population times per capita poverty deficit in US$ billions)
1	Syrian Arab Republic	1,400	1,382	18	19.03	342.55
2	Bhutan	1,400	1,325	75	0.60	45.28
3	Indonesia	1,400	1,302	98	220.58	21,617.20
4	Congo	1,400	1,273	127	4.01	508.80
5	Paraguay	1,400	1,242	158	5.88	928.66
6	Egypt	1,400	1,207	193	74.07	14,295.11
7	Sri Lanka	1,400	1,196	204	19.65	4,008.36
8	Philippines	1,400	1,192	208	83.05	17,275.17
9	Honduras	1,400	1,151	249	7.21	1,795.57

Table 2.3 continued

Table 2.3 continued

No.	Country	Poverty line (US$)	Per capita GDP (US$)	Per capita deficit (poverty line-per capita GDP in US$)	Population (millions)	Total poverty deficit (population times per capita poverty deficit in US$ billions)
10	Occupied Palestinian Territories	1,400	1,107	293	3.61	1,058.72
11	Guyana	1,400	1,048	352	0.76	268.70
12	Cameroon	1,400	1,034	366	16.34	5,982.01
13	Bolivia	1,400	1,017	383	9.14	3,502.36
14	Nicaragua	1,400	954	446	5.14	2,290.78
15	Côte d'Ivoire	1,400	900	500	18.11	9,055.56
16	Djibouti	1,400	894	506	0.78	396.20
17	Papua New Guinea	1,400	840	560	5.83	3,266.67
18	Lesotho	1,400	808	592	1.86	1,099.01
19	Sudan	1,400	760	640	36.18	23,157.89
20	Nigeria	1,400	752	648	131.65	85,308.51
21	Mongolia	1,400	736	664	2.58	1,714.13
22	India	1,400	736	664	1,094.70	72,6881.52
23	Yemen	1,400	718	682	21.03	14,342.90
24	Pakistan	1,400	711	689	155.70	107,274.68
25	Senegal	1,400	707	693	11.60	8,037.62
26	Moldova	1,400	694	706	4.18	2,950.14
27	Comoros	1,400	645	755	0.62	468.22
28	Viet Nam	1,400	631	769	83.04	63,859.90
29	Solomon Islands	1,400	624	776	0.48	373.08
30	Zambia	1,400	623	777	11.72	9,104.49
31	Mauritania	1,400	603	797	3.15	2,511.28
32	Chad	1,400	561	839	9.80	8,225.49
33	Kenya	1,400	547	853	34.19	29,161.06

Table 2.3 continued

Table 2.3 continued

No. Country	Poverty line (US$)	Per capita GDP (US$)	Per capita deficit (poverty line-per capita GDP in US$)	Population (millions)	Total poverty deficit (population times per capita poverty deficit in US$ billions)
34 Uzbekistan	1,400	533	867	26.27	22,772.98
35 Benin	1,400	508	892	8.46	7,550.39
36 Haiti	1,400	500	900	8.60	7,740.00
37 Lao People's Democratic Republic	1,400	485	915	5.98	5,471.13
38 Ghana	1,400	485	915	22.06	20,186.60
39 Kyrgyzstan	1,400	475	925	5.05	4,673.68
40 Sao Tome and Principe	1,400	451	949	0.22	210.42
41 Cambodia	1,400	440	960	14.09	13,527.27
42 Bangladesh	1,400	423	977	141.84	138,581.56
43 Mali	1,400	392	1,008	13.52	13,628.57
44 Burkina Faso	1,400	391	1,009	13.30	13,418.93
45 Timor-Leste	1,400	358	1,042	0.84	873.18
46 Togo	1,400	358	1,042	6.15	6,403.35
47 Tajikistan	1,400	355	1,045	6.48	6,770.42
48 Guinea	1,400	350	1,050	9.43	9,900.00
49 Central African Republic	1,400	339	1,061	4.13	4,381.71
50 Mozambique	1,400	335	1,065	19.70	20,982.09
51 Tanzania (United Republic of)	1,400	316	1,084	38.29	41,507.59
52 Gambia	1,400	304	1,096	1.64	1,802.63
53 Uganda	1,400	303	1,097	28.71	31,498.02
54 Nepal	1,400	272	1,128	27.21	30,688.24
55 Madagascar	1,400	271	1,129	18.45	20,830.26
56 Zimbabwe	1,400	259	1,141	13.13	14,978.38

Table 2.3 continued

Table 2.3 continued

No.	Country	Poverty line (US$)	Per capita GDP (US$)	Per capita deficit (poverty line-per capita GDP in US$)	Population (millions)	Total poverty deficit (population times per capita poverty deficit in US$ billions)
57	Niger	1,400	244	1,156	13.93	16,108.20
58	Rwanda	1,400	238	1,162	9.24	10,741.18
59	Eritrea	1,400	220	1,180	4.55	5,363.64
60	Sierra Leone	1,400	216	1,184	5.56	6,577.78
61	Guinea-Bissau	1,400	190	1,210	1.58	1,910.53
62	Malawi	1,400	161	1,239	13.04	16,160.87
63	Ethiopia	1,400	157	1,243	71.34	88,672.61
64	Congo (Democratic Republic of the)	1,400	123	1,277	57.72	73,713.01
65	Burundi	1,400	106	1,294	7.55	9,766.04
	Aggregate		722.68	677.32	2,714	1,838.50

Source: Derived from Tables 1 and 2 of this paper.
Note: A 'poor country' is one with a per capita GDP of less than 1,400 US$.

The International Burden of Poverty

As we have seen, the aggregate poverty deficit, D, is in the region of 1,839 billion US dollars. From Table 2.1, it can be verified that the aggregate GDP of all the non-poor countries—call this Y—is in the region of 42,082 billion US dollars. The ratio of D to Y is 4.4 per cent, a number scarcely suggestive of an insuperable burden of international poverty. Indeed, the Brandt Commission on North–South Relations, in 1980, had recommended an international tax-cum-transfer arrangement, and it is worth considering the simple arithmetic of eradicating global poverty through aid disbursements consistent with the implementation of a specific scheme of redistributive taxation, as discussed below.

Suppose the objective is to ensure that every presently poor country is enabled to reach the poverty line of 1,400 US dollars per capita. What would be a maximally equitable tax-transfer scheme which will realize this objective, in the sense of ensuring that the resulting global distribution of income cannot be 'Lorenz-dominated', as economists put it, by any other distribution in which the presently poor countries are just enabled to escape poverty? This problem has been considered by Jayaraj and Subramanian (1996) in the context of *within*-country poverty eradication. The solution to the problem can be described as follows. Let the per capita income of the richest country be reduced to that of the next richest country. If the resulting tax revenue is sufficient to meet the aggregate poverty deficit D, then that is all that needs to be done. If not, reduce the per capita incomes of the two richest countries to the per capita income of the third richest country. If the resulting tax revenue is sufficient to meet the deficit D, then the exercise stops at this stage. If not, the per capita incomes of the three richest countries should be reduced to the level of the fourth richest country's per capita income and so on, down the line, until we reach that marginal country for which the aggregate revenue raised is just equal to the aggregate poverty deficit D. What is entailed is the implementation of a 'lexicographic maximin' solution—'L–M scheme', for short—to the optimal taxation problem.[5] (For discussion of a related, though distinct, problem, see Anand's [1983] 'Redressal of Poverty Rule'.)

The tax-cum-transfer scheme just described can, as it happens, be interpreted as reflecting an 'agglomerative' view of three principles of distributive justice—those of 'sufficientarianism' (on which see, in particular, Frankfurt 1987), 'prioritarianism' (on which see, in particular, Parfit 1998), and 'egalitarianism'. (This was pointed out to the author in personal communication by Sanjay Reddy.) Sufficientarianism is, essentially, the view that inequality in itself is objectionable only when, and to the extent that, it coexists with the failure of some people to achieve a standard of living that is compatible with adequacy, or sufficiency, or freedom from need. Prioritarianism is the view that just distribution should be informed by the desirability of attaching greater weight, or priority, to those that are worse off. Egalitarianism is an expression of the belief that an equal distribution of benefits is, in itself, good, or that striving for equality, on grounds of justice or fairness (or some other value), is the right thing to do. That the L–M scheme is compatible with these three principles of distributive justice is not hard to see. If 'sufficiency' in income space is identified with the attainment of a 'poverty line' level of income, then the L–M scheme can be seen to be compatible with sufficientarianism in the sense of supporting a pattern of redistribution which ensures inequality is reduced to the extent that those that are currently poor are just enabled to escape poverty. The L–M scheme is prioritarian in the sense that priority is accorded only to the poor, and, among the poor, greater weight is attached to the poorer, as reflected in the fact that transfers are greater for those with larger poverty deficits, and zero for the non-poor. The demands of egalitarianism are served by the L–M scheme in the following restricted sense: the objective of raising all those who are poor to the poverty line by redistribution is accomplished by the L–M scheme through a pattern of income distribution that cannot be Lorenz dominated by any other scheme of redistribution. The L–M scheme, thus, would appear to be rationalizable in terms of the 'moral mathematics' (a phrase due to Sanjay Reddy 2007) of redistribution that can be derived from each of the principles of sufficientarianism, prioritarianism, and egalitarianism.

Using the data provided in Table 2.1, it can be verified that only the richest 11 countries of the world—Luxembourg, Norway, Iceland, Qatar, Switzerland, Ireland, Denmark, USA, Sweden, Netherlands, and Austria—would be involved in the redistributive exercise described above. The per capita incomes of these countries would have to be reduced to 37,045 US dollars, just a little below the Austrian per capita income of 37,175 US dollars. The details are provided in Table 2.4, and the figures in this table suggest the following.

The post-tax-cum-transfer per capita GDP of the seven richest countries taken together will be over 87 per cent of their pre-tax-cum-transfer per capita GDP, whereas the post-tax-cum-transfer per capita GDP of the 65 poorest countries taken together will be over 193 per cent of their pre-tax-cum-transfer per capita GDP. From an impartial, 'arithmetical' point of view, a relatively small

Table 2.4
Redistributive Taxation for Eradicating Global Poverty, 2005: The 'Lexicographic Maximin' Solution

No.	Country	Per capita GDP (US$)	Income level (x*) to which per capita GDP must be reduced (US$)	Per capita tax (per capita GDP—x*) (US$)	Population (millions)	Total tax (per capita tax times population) (US$ billions)	GDP (US$ billions)	Tax—GD ratio (per cent)
1	Luxembourg	79,851	37,045	42,806	0.4571	19.57	36.5	53.62
2	Norway	63,918	37,045	26,873	4.6231	124.24	295.5	42.04
3	Iceland	53,290	37,045	16,245	0.2965	4.82	15.8	30.49
4	Qatar	52,240	37,045	15,195	0.8136	12.36	42.5	29.09
5	Switzerland	49,351	37,045	12,306	7.4365	91.51	367.0	24.94
6	Ireland	48,524	37,045	11,479	4.1588	47.74	201.8	23.66
7	Denmark	47,769	37,045	10,724	5.4156	58.08	258.7	22.45
8	United States	41,890	37,045	4,845	296.4073	1,436.09	12,416.5	11.57
9	Sweden	39,637	37,045	2,592	9.0244	23.39	357.7	6.54
10	Netherlands	38,248	37,045	1,203	16.3198	19.63	624.2	3.15
11	Austria	37,175	37,045	130	8.2340	1.07	306.1	0.35
	Aggregate					1,838.5	14,922.3	12.32

Source: Derived from Tables 2.1, 2.2, and 2.3.
Note: The quantity $x*$ is defined in endnote 4 (to put it precisely: for every $i \in Q$, $D_i \equiv p_i(z - x_i)$, and $D = \sum_{i \in Q} D_i$).

sacrifice by a small number of rich countries could yield a disproportionately large benefit to a large number of poor countries. The
size of the population in the 'sacrificing' countries is 353 million,
or 13 per cent of the size of the population, at 2,714 million, of the
beneficiary countries. There need be no fear that the transfers will
be anything like remotely immiserizing: at the end of the redistributive exercise, the 11 richest countries will enjoy an average
standard of living very near that of Austria; and the per capita GDP
of the richest country (37,045 US dollars) will still exceed the per
capita GDP of the poorest country (1,400 US dollars) by a factor
of over 2,600 per cent.

The upshot of the preceding discussion leads us to our

> *Third Observation: While the magnitude of global poverty is large, the inter-*
> *national burden of poverty is small.*

The Disbursement of Aid in Relation to Donor Capability

The redistributive tax system described in the previous section
could attract the criticism of being extreme in its insistence on a
certain sort of stringent egalitarianism. In this scheme, only 11 of
the richest countries are called upon to bear the burden of international poverty. In particular, only countries with a per capita GDP
equalling or exceeding the Austrian per capita GDP of 37,175 US
dollars are required to disburse aid. There may well be a case for
a more broad-based spreading of the overheads of global deprivation. The criterion for 'aid liability' can be significantly relaxed—
by requiring, for instance, that the burden of aid should be borne
by countries with a per capita GDP in excess of 14,000 US dollars
(which is itself 10 times the international poverty line of 1,400 US
dollars). Let A be the set of these countries. For every country i in
the set A, let S_i be *country i's surplus*, or the total excess of income
over what it would be if its per capita GDP was exactly equal to
the cut-off level of 14,000 US dollars. The *aggregate global surplus*,
S, is then obtained by summing the surpluses of all countries in the

set A.[6] A reasonably equitable scheme of taxation would be one in which, from among the set A of rich countries, the ith poorest country's share in total aid disbursed is s_i, where $s_i = S_i / S$. That is, a country's share in aid disbursed is equated to its share in the aggregate surplus. One could refer to s_i as country i's 'normative share' in aid disbursement.

Table 2.1 indicates that there are 35 countries constituting the set A: Luxembourg, Norway, Iceland, Qatar, Switzerland, Ireland, Denmark, United States, Sweden, Netherlands, Austria, Finland, United Kingdom, Australia, Japan, Belgium, France, Canada, Germany, Kuwait, Italy, United Arab Emirates, Singapore, New Zealand, Spain, Hong Kong China (SAR), Cyprus, Greece, Israel, Bahrain, Bahamas, Portugal, Slovenia, Brunei Darussalam, and Republic of Korea. Of these, 22 countries belong to the DAC of the OECD. The *HDR 2007–08* (Table 17) furnishes information for 2005 on the aid disbursed by each of the DAC countries. Using these data, and data provided in Table 2.1, Table 2.5 in this paper presents information, for each of the DAC countries, on its actual share a_i of aid disbursed by the DAC countries, and its normative share s_i. The figures in this table suggest that for all but 5 of the 22 DAC countries, the actual aid share a_i is in excess of the normative share s_i: of salience are the cases of Sweden, Netherlands, Norway, and Denmark, for each of which countries the ratio of a_i to s_i is in excess of 2. New Zealand, Ireland, Japan, Australia, and the United States are the countries for which the ratio of a_i to s_i is less than unity. Particularly noteworthy, and for reasons opposite to those which make the Nordic countries remarkable, is the case of the United States, whose actual aid share is just 63 per cent of its normative share. Indeed, at the levels of aid commitment of New Zealand, Ireland, Japan, Australia, and the United States, if the remaining DAC countries decided to disburse aid in accordance with their normative shares, then the total aid disbursement of the DAC countries would be just a little over four-fifths of the present (and already low) level. Clearly, a disproportionate aid effort has had to be put in by one group of countries in order to offset the aid reluctance of countries such as the United States and Australia

Table 2.5
Actual and Normative Aid Shares in Disbursement for the DAC Countries, 2005

No.	Country	Per capita GDP (US$)	Per capita surplus (per capita GDP— 1,400) (US$)	Population (millions)	Total surplus (population times per capita surplus) (US$ billions)	Aid disbursed (US$ billions)	Actual share in aid disbursed (aid disbursed/aggregate aid disbursed) (per cent)	Normative share in aid disbursed (total surplus/ aggregate total surplus) (per cent)	Actual share/ normative share
1	Norway	63,918	49,918	4.6231	230.78	2.79	2.6092	1.1527	2.2635
2	Australia	36,032	22,032	20.3292	447.89	1.68	1.5734	2.2372	0.7033
3	Canada	34,484	20,484	32.2990	661.61	3.76	3.5176	3.3047	1.0644
4	Ireland	48,524	34,524	4.1588	143.58	0.72	0.6734	0.7172	0.9389
5	Sweden	39,637	25,637	9.0244	231.36	3.36	3.1486	1.1556	2.7246
6	Japan	35,484	21,484	127.7759	2,745.14	13.15	12.3127	13.7119	0.8980
7	Netherlands	38,248	24,248	16.3198	395.72	5.12	4.7904	1.9766	2.4235
8	France	34,936	20,936	60.8713	1,274.40	10.03	9.3898	6.3656	1.4751
9	Finland	36,820	22,820	5.2471	119.74	0.90	0.8448	0.5981	1.4124
10	United States	41,890	27,890	296.4073	8,266.80	27.62	25.8691	41.2925	0.6265
11	Spain	25,914	11,914	43.3974	517.04	3.02	2.8265	2.5826	1.0944
12	Denmark	47,769	33,769	5.4156	182.88	2.11	1.9752	0.9135	2.1622
13	Austria	37,175	23,175	8.2340	190.82	1.57	1.4732	0.9532	1.5456

Table 2.5 continued

Table 2.5 continued

No.	Country	Per capita GDP (US$)	Per capita surplus (per capita GDP—1,400) (US$)	Population (millions)	Total surplus (population times per capita surplus) (US$ billions)	Aid disbursed (US$ billions)	Actual share in aid disbursed (aid disbursed/aggregate aid disbursed) (per cent)	Normative share in aid disbursed (total surplus/aggregate total surplus) (per cent)	Actual share/normative share
14	United Kingdom	36,509	22,509	60.2262	1,355.63	10.77	10.0837	6.7714	1.4892
15	Belgium	35,389	21,389	10.4778	224.11	1.96	1.8384	1.1194	1.6423
16	Luxembourg	79,851	65,851	0.4571	30.10	0.26	0.2398	0.1504	1.5946
17	New Zealand	26,664	12,664	4.0992	51.91	0.27	0.2566	0.2593	0.9896
18	Italy	30,073	16,073	58.6074	942.00	5.09	4.7679	4.7053	1.0133
19	Germany	33,890	19,890	82.4698	1640.32	10.08	9.4422	8.1934	1.1524
20	Greece	20,282	6,282	11.1034	69.75	0.38	0.3596	0.3484	1.0322
21	Portugal	17,376	3,376	10.5490	35.61	0.38	0.3531	0.1779	1.9848
22	Switzerland	49,351	35,351	7.4365	262.89	1.77	1.6549	1.3131	1.2603
	Aggregate				20,020.09	106.78			

Source: Derived from Table 2.1 and Table 17 of HDR 2007–08.

which account, respectively, for the highest and the next highest share in the aggregate global surplus. This leads us to our

Fourth Observation: The relative contributions to aid bear little relation to the relative capabilities of donor countries.

The Receipt of Aid in Relation to Beneficiary Need

Bourguignon and Fields (1990)—see also Gangopadhyay and Subramanian (1992)—are one of the earliest efforts at engaging explicitly with the question of optimal budgetary intervention in the alleviation of poverty. Their approach can be adapted to the context of an aid allocation exercise. Specifically, if a budget B is available for aid disbursement, and if the objective of aid transfers is to minimize poverty, how much aid B_i should be allocated to the *i*th poorest country in the set of poor countries? The answer would depend on how one specifies the objective function (or equivalently, in the present case, on how one measures poverty) and also on the constraints under which the optimization exercise is carried out. Bourguignon and Fields (as adapted to our present concerns) consider different members of the Foster–Greer–Thorbecke P_α family of poverty measures, and they seek to minimize poverty as measured by each of these indices subject to the constraints (a) that the sum of aid transfers does not exceed the budgeted outlay B, (b) that no country receives aid in excess of its poverty deficit, and (c) that aid transfers are always non–negative. Suppose we add a mildly 'equality-preferring' fourth constraint which demands that for every pair of poor countries, the share of the poorer country in the combined poverty deficit of the pair should not become larger after the aid transfers have been made. Effectively, this constraint is compatible with the requirement that the poorer (in terms of poverty deficit) of two countries should not receive a smaller transfer. Suppose, further, that poverty is measured by the index $P_{0.5}$, Subramanian (2006) has demonstrated that the solution to this constrained optimization problem is a *proportional allocation rule*, whereby each country receives aid in proportion to its share in the aggregate poverty deficit. That is, the share d_i of the ith poorest country in the budgeted outlay of B will simply be the country's share in the aggregate poverty deficit, namely, the quantity D_i/D.[7]

The proportionality rule just described is, we shall maintain, a reasonably rational guide to aid-allocation decisions. It should be mentioned here that Milanovic (2006) has advanced a proposal for the creation of an independent international agency to preside over the global redistribution of income. The schedule of aid disbursement by donor countries (reviewed in the preceding section) and the schedule of aid receipts by recipient countries (reviewed in this section) are examples of elementary rules in terms of which Milanovic's proposed international agency could be guided in its global redistribution exercise.

We shall refer to d_i as country i's *normative share* in aid receipts. How has the pattern of *actual* country shares in aid receipts—call these the b_i—compared with the normative shares? Table 2.6 of this paper, based on 2005 data available in Table 18 of the *HDR 2007–08*, furnishes information on the amount of aid received by each country for which data are available on GDP, population, and aid receipt. (It is to be noted that of the total aid disbursement of 110 billion US dollars in 2005, only about 54 per cent—or 59.3 billion US dollars—have been allocated as receipts to specific countries.) Table 2.6 reveals that if a poverty line of 1,400 US dollars per capita is accepted as an international poverty line, then as many as 60 *non-poor* countries out of a total of 125 countries have been recipients of positive net aid. Specific examples thrown up by Table 2.6 are worth noting. If we describe a country by an ordered pair of per capita GDP and per capita aid received, then here are some pairs of numbers for selected countries, which suggest that it would be hard to find any need-related rationale for aid allocations. (The suggestion, it may be clarified, is not that the precise disproportionalities reported in what follows for the year 2005 are reflective of some secular pattern that is replicated on a year-to-year basis. That is, the claim is about a certain generic inter-temporal commonality of idiosyncratic aid receipts without, necessarily, a specific inter-temporal identity of country-wise patterns.) Grenada,

Table 2.6

Aid, Income, and Poverty Deficit Data for All Aid-receiving Countries, 2005

No.	Country	Per capita GDP (US$)	Per capita deficit (poverty line—per capita GDP in US$)	Population (millions)	Total poverty deficit (population times per capita poverty deficit in US$ millions)	Aid receipt (US$ millions)
(A) Non-poor countries						
1	Saudi Arabia	13,399	-11,999	23.1211	-277,430.42	26.3
2	Barbados	11,465	-10,065	0.2704	-2,721.46	-2.1
3	Trinidad and Tobago	11,000	-9,600	1.3091	-12,567.27	-2.1
4	Antigua and Barbuda	10,578	-9,178	0.0851	-780.88	7.2
5	Oman	9,584	-8,184	2.5355	-20,750.33	30.7
6	Saint Kitts and Nevis	9,438	-8,038	0.0530	-425.83	3.5
7	Croatia	8,666	-7,266	4.4426	-32,280.29	125.4
8	Seychelles	8,209	-6,809	0.0853	-580.62	18.8
9	Mexico	7,454	-6,054	103.0856	-624,080.17	189.4
10	Chile	7,073	-5,673	16.2873	-92,397.79	151.7
11	Libyan Arab Jamahiriya	6,621	-5,221	5.8601	-30,595.80	24.4
12	Equatorial Guinea	6,416	-5,016	0.4988	-2,501.75	39.0
13	Lebanon	6,135	-4,735	3.5697	-16,902.44	243.0
14	Botswana	5,846	-4,446	1.7619	-7,833.36	70.9
15	Gabon	5,821	-4,421	1.3915	-6,151.88	53.9
16	Venezuela (Bolivarian Republic of)	5,275	-3,875	26.5782	-102,990.52	48.7
17	Malaysia	5,142	-3,742	25.3403	-94,823.53	31.6
18	South Africa	5,109	-3,709	46.8781	-173,870.72	700.0
19	Mauritius	5,059	-3,659	1.2453	-4,556.57	31.9
20	Turkey	5,030	-3,630	72.0676	-261,605.37	464.0

Table 2.6 continued

Table 2.6 continued

No.	Country	Per capita GDP (US$)	Per capita deficit (poverty line—per capita GDP in US$)	Population (millions)	Total poverty deficit (population times per capita poverty deficit in US$ millions)	Aid receipt (US$ millions)
21	Saint Lucia	5,007	-3,607	0.1598	-576.31	11.1
22	Uruguay	4,848	-3,448	3.4653	-11,948.51	14.6
23	Panama	4,786	-3,386	3.2386	-10,965.94	19.5
24	Argentina	4,728	-3,328	38.7479	-128,952.96	99.7
25	Costa Rica	4,627	-3,227	4.3225	-13,948.56	29.5
26	Grenada	4,451	-3,051	0.1123	-342.73	44.9
27	Brazil	4,271	-2,871	186.3966	-535,144.72	191.9
28	Dominica	3,938	-2,538	0.0762	-193.35	15.2
29	Belize	3,786	-2,386	0.2905	-693.24	12.9
30	Kazakhstan	3,772	-2,372	15.1379	-35,907.00	229.2
31	Saint Vincent and the Grenadines	3,612	-2,212	0.1107	-244.96	4.9
32	Jamaica	3,607	-2,207	2.6615	-5,873.91	35.7
33	Dominican Republic	3,317	-1,917	8.8936	-17,048.99	77.0
34	Fiji	3,219	-1,819	0.8388	-1,525.72	64.0
35	Algeria	3,112	-1,712	32.8728	-56,278.15	370.6
36	Belarus	3,024	-1,624	9.7884	-15,896.30	53.8
37	Namibia	3,016	-1,616	2.0225	-3,268.44	123.4
38	Suriname	2,986	-1,586	0.4354	-690.49	44.0
39	Tunisia	2,860	-1,460	10.0350	-14,651.05	376.5
40	Peru	2,838	-1,438	27.9774	-40,231.57	397.8
41	Macedonia (TFYR)	2,835	-1,435	2.0459	-2,935.80	230.3
42	Iran (Islamic Republic of)	2,781	-1381	68.2488	-94,251.64	104.0
43	Ecuador	2,758	-1,358	13.2342	-17,972.08	209.5
44	Thailand	2,750	-1,350	64.2182	-86,694.55	-171.1

Table 2.6 continued

Table 2.6 continued

No.	Country	Per capita GDP (US$)	Per capita deficit (poverty line—per capita GDP in US$)	Population (millions)	Total poverty deficit (population times per capita poverty deficit in US$ millions)	Aid receipt (US$ millions)
45	Colombia	2,682	−1,282	45.6003	−58,459.58	511.1
46	Albania	2,678	−1,278	3.1367	−4,008.66	318.7
47	Bosnia and Herzegovina	2,546	−1,146	3.8885	−4,456.17	546.1
48	Guatemala	2,517	−1,117	12.5944	−14,067.90	253.6
49	El Salvador	2,467	−1,067	6.8910	−7,352.66	199.4
50	Swaziland	2,414	−1,014	1.1185	−1,134.13	46.0
51	Maldives	2,326	−926	0.3439	−318.49	66.8
52	Jordan	2,323	−923	5.4671	−5,046.10	622.0
53	Samoa	2,184	−784	0.1832	−143.59	44.0
54	Tonga	2,090	−690	0.0957	−66.03	31.8
55	Angola	2,058	−658	15.9378	−10,487.07	441.8
56	Cape Verde	1,940	−540	0.5155	−278.35	160.6
57	Ukraine	1,761	−361	47.0755	−16,994.26	409.6
58	China	1,713	−313	1,304.3199	−408,252.13	1,756.9
59	Morocco	1,711	−311	30.1578	−9,379.08	651.8
60	Turkmenistan	1,669	−269	4.8532	−1,305.51	28.3
61	Armenia	1,625	−225	3.0154	−678.46	193.3
62	Azerbaijan	1,498	−98	8.4112	−824.30	223.4
63	Georgia	1,429	−29	4.4787	−129.88	309.8
	Aggregate			2,329.9		11,660.1
(B) Poor countries						
1	Syrian Arab Republic	1,382	18	19.0304	342.55	77.9
2	Bhutan	1,325	75	0.6038	45.28	90.0
3	Indonesia	1,302	98	220.5837	21,617.20	2,523.5
4	Congo	1,273	127	4.0063	508.80	1,448.9
5	Paraguay	1,242	158	5.8776	928.66	51.1

Table 2.6 continued

Table 2.6 continued

No.	Country	Per capita GDP (US$)	Per capita deficit (poverty line—per capita GDP in US$)	Population (millions)	Total poverty deficit (population times per capita poverty deficit in US$ millions)	Aid receipt (US$ millions)
6	Egypt	1,207	193	74.0679	14,295.11	925.9
7	Sri Lanka	1,196	204	19.6488	4,008.36	1,189.3
8	Philippines	1,192	208	83.0537	17,275.17	561.8
9	Honduras	1,151	249	7.2111	1,795.57	680.8
10	Occupied Palestinian Territories	1,107	293	3.6134	1,058.72	1,101.6
11	Guyana	1,048	352	0.7634	268.70	136.8
12	Cameroon	1,034	366	16.3443	5,982.01	413.8
13	Bolivia	1,017	383	9.1445	3,502.36	582.9
14	Nicaragua	954	446	5.1363	2,290.78	740.1
15	Côte d'Ivoire	900	500	18.1111	9,055.56	119.1
16	Djibouti	894	506	0.7830	396.20	78.6
17	Papua New Guinea	840	560	5.8333	3,266.67	266.1
18	Lesotho	808	592	1.8564	1,099.01	68.8
19	Sudan	760	640	36.1842	23,157.89	1,828.6
20	Nigeria	752	648	131.6489	85,308.51	6,437.3
21	Mongolia	736	664	2.5815	1,714.13	211.9
22	India	736	664	1,094.7011	726,881.52	1,724.1
23	Yemen	718	682	21.0306	14,342.90	335.9
24	Pakistan	711	689	155.6962	107,274.68	1,666.5
25	Senegal	707	693	11.5983	8,037.62	689.3
26	Moldova	694	706	4.1787	2,950.14	191.8
27	Comoros	645	755	0.6202	468.22	25.2
28	Viet Nam	631	769	83.0428	63,859.90	1,904.9
29	Solomon Islands	624	776	0.4808	373.08	198.2

Table 2.6 continued

Table 2.6 continued

No.	Country	Per capita GDP (US$)	Per capita deficit (poverty line—per capita GDP in US$)	Population (millions)	Total poverty deficit (population times per capita poverty deficit in US$ millions)	Aid receipt (US$ millions)
30	Zambia	623	777	11.7175	9,104.49	945.0
31	Mauritania	603	797	3.1509	2,511.28	190.4
32	Chad	561	839	9.8039	8,225.49	379.8
33	Kenya	547	853	34.1865	29,161.06	768.3
34	Uzbekistan	533	867	26.2664	22,772.98	172.3
35	Benin	508	892	8.4646	7,550.39	349.1
36	Haiti	500	900	8.6000	7,740.00	515.0
37	Lao People's Democratic Republic	485	915	5.9794	5,471.13	295.7
38	Ghana	485	915	22.0619	20,186.60	1,119.9
39	Kyrgyzstan	475	925	5.0526	4,673.68	268.5
40	Sao Tome and Principe	451	949	0.2217	210.42	31.9
41	Cambodia	440	960	14.0909	13,527.27	537.8
42	Bangladesh	423	977	141.8440	138,581.56	1,320.5
43	Mali	392	1008	13.5204	13,628.57	691.5
44	Burkina Faso	391	1,009	13.2992	13,418.93	659.6
45	Togo	358	1,042	6.1453	6,403.35	86.7
46	Timor-Leste	358	1,042	0.8380	873.18	184.7
47	Tajikistan	355	1,045	6.4789	6,770.42	241.4
48	Guinea	350	1,050	9.4286	9,900.00	182.1
49	Central African Republic	339	1,061	4.1298	4,381.71	95.3
50	Mozambique	335	1,065	19.7015	20,982.09	1,285.9
51	Tanzania (United Republic of)	316	1,084	38.2911	41,507.59	1,505.1
52	Gambia	304	1,096	1.6447	1,802.63	58.2
53	Uganda	303	1,097	28.7129	31,498.02	1,198.0

Table 2.6 continued

Table 2.6 continued

No.	Country	Per capita GDP (US$)	Per capita deficit (poverty line—per capita GDP in US$)	Population (millions)	Total poverty deficit (population times per capita poverty deficit in US$ millions)	Aid receipt (US$ millions)
54	Nepal	272	1,128	27.2059	30,688.24	427.9
55	Madagascar	271	1,129	18.4502	20,830.26	929.2
56	Zimbabwe	259	1,141	13.1274	14,978.38	367.7
57	Niger	244	1,156	13.9344	16,108.20	515.4
58	Rwanda	238	1,162	9.2437	10,741.18	576.0
59	Eritrea	220	1,180	4.5455	5,363.64	355.2
60	Sierra Leone	216	1,184	5.5556	6,577.78	343.4
61	Guinea-Bissau	190	1,210	1.5789	1,910.53	79.1
62	Malawi	161	1,239	13.0435	16,160.87	575.3
63	Ethiopia	157	1,243	71.3376	88,672.61	1,937.3
64	Congo (Democratic Republic of the)	123	1,277	57.7236	73,713.01	1,827.6
65	Burundi	106	1,294	7.5472	9,766.04	365.0
	Aggregate			2,714.4		47,652.5

Source: Derived from Table 2.1.
Note: A 'poor country' is one with a per capita GDP of less than 1,400 US dollars.

with a per capita GDP of 4,451 US dollars, receives a per capita aid of 400 US dollars, and Croatia, with a per capita GDP of 8,666 US dollars, receives a per capita aid of 28 US dollars: both of these are non-poor countries. Contrast these figures with those for a pair of poor countries: India, with a per capita GDP of 736 US dollars, receives a per capita aid of 1.58 US dollars, while Pakistan, with a per capita GDP of 711 US dollars, receives a per capita aid of 4.43 US dollars. Grenada's per capita GDP is nearly 12 times that of India, whereas India's aid receipt per capita is 0.056 times that of Grenada.

Finally, and confining ourselves to the set of poor countries, it is instructive to look at the pattern of actual shares b_i in aid receipts in relation to the corresponding normative shares d_i. Table 2.7 presents the relevant information. A generous margin of deviation from unity of the actual-to-normative-share ratio would be the interval (0.5, 1.5). As it happens, and as Table 2.7 reveals, only 20 of the 65 poor countries fall within this band. For the rest, we have a wide range of variation in the ratio of actual aid share to normative aid share, with the polarities described by Congo (110) at one end of the spectrum, and Uzbekistan (0.09) at the other end.

In the light of the preceding discussion, we are led to our

> *Fifth Observation: The relative receipts of aid bear little relation to the relative needs of beneficiary countries.*

Table 2.7

Actual and Normative Aid Shares of Aid-receiving Poor Countries, 2005

No.	Country	Total poverty deficit (from Table 2.6) in US$ millions	Aid receipt (US$ millions)	Actual share in aid received (aid received/ aggregate aid received) (per cent)	Normative share in aid received (total deficit/ aggregate total deficit) (per cent)	Actual aid share/ normative aid share
1	Congo	508.80	1,448.90	3.04	0.03	109.87
2	Bhutan	45.28	90.00	0.19	0.00	76.68
3	Occupied Palestinian Territories	1,058.72	1,101.60	2.31	0.06	40.14
4	Solomon Islands	373.08	198.20	0.42	0.02	20.50
5	Guyana	268.70	136.80	0.29	0.01	19.64
6	Honduras	1,795.57	680.80	1.43	0.10	14.63
7	Nicaragua	2,290.78	740.10	1.55	0.12	12.46
8	Sri Lanka	4,008.36	1,189.30	2.50	0.22	11.45
9	Syrian Arab Republic	342.55	77.90	0.16	0.02	8.77
10	Timor-Leste	873.18	184.70	0.39	0.05	8.16

Table 2.7 continued

Table 2.7 continued

No.	Country	Total poverty deficit (from Table 2.6) in US$ millions	Aid receipt (US$ millions)	Actual share in aid received (aid received / aggregate aid received) (per cent)	Normative share in aid received (total deficit / aggregate total deficit) (per cent)	Actual aid share / normative aid share
11	Djibouti	396.20	78.60	0.16	0.02	7.65
12	Bolivia	3,502.36	582.90	1.22	0.19	6.42
13	Sao Tome and Principe	210.42	31.90	0.07	0.01	5.85
14	Mongolia	1,714.13	211.90	0.44	0.09	4.77
15	Indonesia	21,617.20	2,523.50	5.30	1.18	4.50
16	Zambia	9,104.49	945.00	1.98	0.50	4.00
17	Senegal	8,037.62	689.30	1.45	0.44	3.31
18	Papua New Guinea	3,266.67	266.10	0.56	0.18	3.14
19	Sudan	23,157.89	1,828.60	3.84	1.26	3.05
20	Mauritania	2,511.28	190.40	0.40	0.14	2.93
21	Nigeria	85,308.51	6,437.30	13.51	4.64	2.91
22	Cameroon	5,982.01	413.80	0.87	0.33	2.67
23	Haiti	7,740.00	515.00	1.08	0.42	2.57
24	Eritrea	5,363.64	355.20	0.75	0.29	2.56
25	Moldova	2,950.14	191.80	0.40	0.16	2.51
26	Egypt	14,295.11	925.90	1.94	0.78	2.50
27	Lesotho	1,099.01	68.80	0.14	0.06	2.42
28	Mozambique	20,982.09	1,285.90	2.70	1.14	2.36
29	Kyrgyzstan	4,673.68	268.50	0.56	0.25	2.22
30	Ghana	20,186.60	1,119.90	2.35	1.10	2.14
31	Paraguay	928.66	51.10	0.11	0.05	2.12
32	Lao People's Democratic Republic	5,471.13	295.70	0.62	0.30	2.09
33	Comoros	468.22	25.20	0.05	0.03	2.08
34	Rwanda	10,741.18	576.00	1.21	0.58	2.07

Table 2.7 continued

Table 2.7 continued

No.	Country	Total poverty deficit (from Table 2.6) in US$ millions	Aid receipt (US$ millions)	Actual share in aid received (aid received/ aggregate aid received) (per cent)	Normative share in aid received (total deficit/ aggregate total deficit) (per cent)	Actual aid share/ normative aid share
35	Sierra Leone	6,577.78	343.40	0.72	0.36	2.01
36	Mali	13,628.57	691.50	1.45	0.74	1.96
37	Burkina Faso	13,418.93	659.60	1.38	0.73	1.90
38	Benin	7,550.39	349.10	0.73	0.41	1.78
39	Chad	8,225.49	379.80	0.80	0.45	1.78
40	Madagascar	20,830.26	929.20	1.95	1.13	1.72
41	Guinea-Bissau	1,910.53	79.10	0.17	0.10	1.60
42	Cambodia	13,527.27	537.80	1.13	0.74	1.53
43	Uganda	31,498.02	1,198.00	2.51	1.71	1.47
44	Burundi	9,766.04	365.00	0.77	0.53	1.44
45	Tanzania (United Republic of)	41,507.59	1,505.10	3.16	2.26	1.40
46	Tajikistan	6,770.42	241.40	0.51	0.37	1.38
47	Malawi	16,160.87	575.30	1.21	0.88	1.37
48	Philippines	17,275.17	561.80	1.18	0.94	1.25
49	Gambia	1,802.63	58.20	0.12	0.10	1.25
50	Niger	16,108.20	515.40	1.08	0.88	1.23
51	Viet Nam	63,859.90	1,904.90	4.00	3.47	1.15
52	Kenya	29,161.06	768.30	1.61	1.59	1.02
53	Congo (Democratic Republic of the)	73,713.01	1,827.60	3.84	4.01	0.96
54	Zimbabwe	14,978.38	367.70	0.77	0.81	0.95
55	Yemen	14,342.90	335.90	0.70	0.78	0.90
56	Ethiopia	88,672.61	1,937.30	4.07	4.82	0.84
57	Central African Republic	4,381.71	95.30	0.20	0.24	0.84

Table 2.7 continued

Table 2.7 continued

No.	Country	Total poverty deficit (from Table 2.6) in US$ millions	Aid receipt (US$ millions)	Actual share in aid received (aid received/ aggregate aid received) (per cent)	Normative share in aid received (total deficit/ aggregate total deficit) (per cent)	Actual aid share/ normative aid share
58	Guinea	9,900.00	182.10	0.38	0.54	0.71
59	Pakistan	107,274.68	1,666.50	3.50	5.83	0.60
60	Nepal	30,688.24	427.90	0.90	1.67	0.54
61	Togo	6,403.35	86.70	0.18	0.35	0.52
62	Côte d'Ivoire	9,055.56	119.10	0.25	0.49	0.51
63	Bangladesh	138,581.56	1,320.50	2.77	7.54	0.37
64	Uzbekistan	22,772.98	172.30	0.36	1.24	0.29
65	India	726,881.52	1,724.10	3.62	39.54	0.09
	Total	1,838,498.89	47,652.50	100.00	100.00	

Source: Derived from Tables 1 and 2 of this paper.
Note: A 'poor country' is one with a per capita GDP of less than 1,400 US$.

Allowing for Intra-country Inequality in the Distribution of Income

It should be stressed that even if the total quantum of aid is equal to the aggregate poverty deficit D, and if actual shares in aid disbursement and aid receipt are precisely equal to their respective normative shares, aid would be a successful means of eradicating global income poverty only on the assumption that there is no intra-country inequality in the distribution of GDP. As a matter of fact, however, per capita GDP for a poor country could rise through an infusion of aid without making much of an impact on poverty if the aid is not employed appropriately to address pre-existing domestic inequality and injustice or is employed in projects—controlled by domestic dictators, for instance—which can exacerbate the mal-distribution of income. By looking only at GDP per capita, one overlooks the problem of targeting aid within the recipient country, and therefore the problem of how to persuade a beneficiary country to attend to a poverty-eradicating distribution of the aid on offer to it—a problem that has often been held out as a reason for the reluctance of wealthy countries to increase the size of overseas development assistance. (This complication has been brought to the author's attention in personal communication by Thomas Pogge.)

One possible way of addressing this complication might be to conceive of an institutional setting in which a special international agency, as prescribed by Milanovic (2006), is fully entrusted with the task of intra-country allocation of aid—even at the apparent cost of interfering with national sovereignty. At an analytical level, the problem of aid allocation can be viewed as a two-stage problem. In the first stage, the concern is with the determination of the country-specific levels of aid provision to be made. A possible formula is the 'proportionality rule' we have already considered. If B is the total quantum of aid available, if D is the aggregate poverty deficit of all the poor countries taken together, and if D_i is the poverty deficit of the ith poorest country, then the proportionality rule will dictate that the allocation to the ith poorest country which will minimize the poverty index $P_{0.5}$ is given by $B_i^* = (D_i/D)B$.

At the second stage of the allocation problem, one can determine the intra-country allocation of the optimal budget B_i^* for the ith poorest country. At this stage of the problem, one can relax the assumption of an equal within-country distribution of incomes and consider the actual (unequal) distribution that obtains. The problem of within-country allocation can now again be setup as a programming exercise. Indeed, and by way of example, the problem to be solved at the intra-national level can be formulated in terms which are formally identical to the way in which the problem was formulated, in the first stage, at the international level. That is to say, if $P_{0.5}^i$ is the poverty level, as measured by the index $P_{0.5}$, of the ith poorest country, the objective could be to minimize $P_{0.5}^i$ subject to the constraints (a) that the sum of aid transfers to country i's citizens does not exceed the country's budgeted outlay B_i^*, (b) that no person receives aid in excess of her poverty deficit, (c) that aid transfers are always non-negative, and (d) that for every pair of poor individuals the share of the poorer person in the combined poverty deficit of the pair should not become larger after the aid transfers have been made. The solution to this problem will, of course, again be the proportionality rule, in a within-country context: no non-poor person will receive any aid, while each poor person will receive aid in proportion to her share in the aggregate poverty shortfall of all the poor persons taken together. The usual problems of information and enforcement cannot, of course, be eliminated in this imperfect world, but presumably the problem of a deliberate, centrally sponsored sub-optimal targeting of benefits can be sought to be minimized. Alternatively, or additionally, one could favour an independent international agency that imposes severe conditionalities on the appropriate internal directing of aid. If the Bretton Woods agencies could successfully impose conditionalities on lending to sustain structural adjustment, it is not clear why conditionalities cannot be imposed—or will not be accepted, especially by the 'radical' constituency of commentators—in the good cause of sensible and scrupulous within-country aid allocation. It would be hard to deny the case for a stringent monitoring of where the aid goes, and for making subsequent rounds of aid severely contingent on past performance. Briefly, the problem of fair and rational intra-country aid allocation need not, in principle, jeopardize the prospect of fair and rational inter-country aid allocation.

Having said this, and so that one does not veer over wholly to the other side, it would be fair to note that, even if aid is abused, this should not entail any overwhelming financial cost for the donor countries: possibly more wheat is dumped in the ocean to keep international prices up than is allocated to aid. In other words, while it is undeniable that some countries would certainly hesitate to offer aid when it simply ends up financing dictators or corrupt governments, it is also true that for many other countries this serves as an alibi for plain flintiness and ungenerosity (especially considering how much is spent in keeping various corrupt regimes going). As Pogge (2003) points out, an important component of what he calls the 'Purely Domestic Poverty Thesis' is the view that it is not so much an unfair global order as the prevalence of corrupt and brutal governments and elites in poor countries which accounts for so much global deprivation: a comforting construction that omits to acknowledge the grave complicity of the world order itself in the corruption and brutality of the systems of power that prevail in many poor countries.

Concluding Observations

As threatened at the outset, this has been an unsubtle paper. There are a number of complications[8] we have not taken on board: the possibility that income is not the only indicator of deprivation; the possibility that there are inter-country variations in the ability to effectively 'absorb' aid; the possibility that aid allocations are sometimes influenced by the historical specificity of events like colonialism which mediate bilateral relations; and, of course, the possibility that rich countries do not see themselves as being under a moral obligation to assist poor countries. In respect of the last complication, an argument that is often held out is that poor countries do not have a *right* to aid. Even setting aside the counter-view that aid is no more than a reparation for historical and contemporary wrongs such as colonialism and unfair trade practices, it is worthwhile to remind oneself of Timmermann's (2004) observation: 'Rights imply duties, but there can be duties without corresponding rights'.

Despite all the direct plainness of the observations made earlier—namely that there is a great deal of poverty in the world; that the quantum of aid available is very small in relation to the magnitude of the poverty problem; that the redistributive effort that would be required to eradicate poverty is quite small; and that there is little relationship between actual and normative aid shares at the dispensing end, and similarly little relationship between actual and normative aid shares at the receiving end—the orders of magnitude reviewed do not suggest that a greater accommodation of complexity will make substantial dents in the truth of these observations. The justification for a certain absence of subtlety derives from the persistence of the truths it reflects. Fussy sophistication in the discourse on aid which does not directly address these stubborn truths could largely be a matter of arranging the deck-chairs, by

remote control, on someone else's *Titanic*. There is no doubt that
the 'moral mathematics' of this paper lack finesse, but it is to be
hoped that they at least assist in preventing one from losing one's
way in exquisite by-lanes.

End Notes

1. Let z stand for the international poverty line, x_i for the per capita GDP of the
   ith poorest country, and p_i for its population. There are m countries, and total
   population is $p \ (= \sum_{i=1}^{m} p_i)$. We let N stand for the set of all countries and Q
   for the set of poor countries, where $Q \equiv \{i \in N \,|\, x_i < z\}$. The cardinality of N is
   m, and that of Q is q. The global distribution of income is represented by the
   partitioned vector $(x; p) = (x_1, \dots , x_m; p_1, \dots , p_m)$, with the countries indexed
   in non-decreasing order of per capita GDP, that is, such that $x_i \le x_{i+1}$, for all i
   $= 1, \dots , m\text{-}1$. For every country i, (x_i, p_i) represents a combination of the per
   capita GDP and population size of that country.
2. For every partitioned vector $(x; p)$ and poverty line z, the P_a family of poverty
   indices is given by

$$P_a ((x; p); z) = \left(\frac{1}{p}\right) \sum_{i \in Q} p_i \left[\frac{z - x_i}{z}\right]^a , \quad a \ge 0.$$

3. To see what is involved, note first that a reduction in a poor person's income
   will leave the number of poor persons, and therefore the headcount ratio (P_0),
   unchanged; however, the average income of the poor will decline, and therefore the per capita income-gap ratio (P_1) will rise, which explains why P_0 fails,
   and P_1 satisfies, the monotonicity condition. A transfer of income from a poor
   person to a poorer one will leave both the headcount ratio and the income-
   gap ratio (or proportionate shortfall of the average income of the poor from
   the poverty line) unchanged (notice that a pure redistribution is not going to
   affect the average income of the poor), which is why the transfer axiom is
   violated by both P_0 and P_1 (which latter is just the product of the headcount
   and the income-gap ratios). If H is the headcount ratio, I the income-gap
   ratio, and C^2 the squared coefficient variation in the distribution of poor incomes—this a well-known summary measure of relative inequality—then it
   can be shown that the poverty index P_2 can be written as: $P_2 = H[I^2 + (1 - I)^2$
   $C^2]$; a progressive income transfer will reduce the value of C^2, and therefore
   of P_2. This poverty measure, consequently, satisfies the transfer axiom. The
   parameter α in the P_a family of indices is a register of 'equity-consciousness:'
   the poverty measure increases in its distribution-sensitivity with an increase in
   α until, in the limit, as α goes to infinity, P_a converges on a sort of 'Rawlsian'
   measure such that distributions are ranked solely by the poverty of the poorest
   individual.
4. To put it precisely: for every $i \in Q, D_i \equiv p_i(z - x_i)$ and $D = \sum_{i \in Q} D_i$.

5. Formally, let $x*$ be a level of income and $q*$ the poorest of the rich countries, such that these are determined through the following equation:

$$\sum_{i=q*}^{m} p_i(x_i - x*) = D.$$

Then, the optimal tax schedule $\{T_i^*\}_{i \in N}$, as described in the text, is given by

$T_i^* = 0 \ \forall i \in \{1, \dots, q* - 1\};$
$\quad = p_i (x_i - x*) \ \forall i \in \{q*, \dots, m\}.$

Under the solution described above, the per capita incomes of the richest $(m - q*)$ countries are equalized, through reduction, to a level of income $x*$ such that the proceeds from this scheme of taxation are just sufficient to bridge the aggregate poverty deficit D.

6. That is, for all $i \in A : S_i \equiv p_i(x_i - 14{,}000)$ and $S = \sum_{i \in A} S_i$.

7. All of this can be stated more formally as follows. Let j and k be two poor countries with aggregate poverty deficits D_j and D_k, respectively. Let $\sigma_{j,k} \equiv D_j / (D_j + D_k)$, that is, $\sigma_{j,k}$ is the share of j in the combined poverty deficits of j and k. Obviously, if $D_j \geq D_k$, then $\sigma_{j,k} \geq \frac{1}{2}$. Let $\sigma'_{j,k}$ be the value of $\sigma_{j,k}$ after the aid transfers have been made. Then, a preference for equality in aid distribution is compatible with the requirement that if j is the country with the larger poverty deficit, the index of pairwise inequality $\sigma_{j,k}$ should not become larger after the distribution, that is, we would require that $\sigma'_{j,k} \leq \sigma_{j,k}$. Let poverty be measured by the index $P_{0.5}$, then the aid allocation problem can be setup formally as a programming exercise of the following type:

(*) Minimize $P_{0.5} (D_1 - B_1, \dots, D_q - B_q; z) = \left(\dfrac{1}{pz^{0.5}}\right) \sum_{i \in Q} (D_i - B_i)^{0.5}$
$\quad \{B_i\}_{i \in Q}$
subject to

(a) $\sum_{i \in Q} B_i \leq B$;

(b) $B_i \leq D_i \ \forall i \in Q$;

(c) $B_i \geq 0 \ \forall i \in Q$; and

(d) $\forall j,k \in Q,$ if $\sigma_{j,k} \geq \frac{1}{2}$, then $\sigma'_{j,k} \leq \sigma_{j,k}$.

Subramanian (2006) has shown that the optimal solution to problem (*) is given by

$$B = d_i B, \text{ where } d_i \equiv \frac{D_i}{D}, \ \forall i \in Q.$$

8. A particular complication not considered in this paper relates to the host of economy-wide macro effects which policies of taxation and transfer can have on both donor and recipient countries. Ram Reddy, in personal correspondence, has pointed out that aid mobilized through income taxation can result in a sort of forced saving for the donor country, and the consequentially altered aggregate saving rate can affect its rate of growth of national income and therefore the dynamics of the patterns and quantum of aid flows. Depending

on how aid is utilized in the recipient country, there could be smaller or larger multiplier effects on income-generation with implications for the magnitude of future flows of aid. Taxation and transfer can also have incentive effects at both the giving and receiving ends of aid, and these are not easy to predict. These, and related issues, are clearly important ones to address in any comprehensive treatment of the subject of aid, but they are somewhat outside the purview of the rather more limited objectives of the present paper.

References

Anand, S. (1983), *Inequality and Poverty in Malaysia: Measurement and Decomposition*. New York: Oxford University Press.

Bourguignon, F. and G.S. Fields. (1990), 'Poverty Measures and Anti-Poverty Policy', *Recherches Economiques de Louvain*, 56: 409–27.

Frankfurt, H. (1987),'Equality as a Moral Ideal', *Ethics*, 98(1): 21-43.

Foster, J.E., J. Greer, and E. Thorbecke. (1984), 'A Class of Decomposable Poverty Measures', *Econometrica*, 52: 761–6.

Gangopadhyay, S. and S. Subramanian. (1992), 'Optimal Budgetary Intervention in Poverty Alleviation Programmes', in S. Subramanian (ed.), *Themes in Development Economics: Essays in Honour of Malcolm Adiseshiah*. New Delhi: Oxford University Press.

Jayaraj, D. and S. Subramanian. (1996), 'Poverty Eradication Through Redistributive Taxation: Some Elementary Considerations', *Review of Development and Change*, 1(1): 73–84.

Milanovic, B. (2006), 'Global Income Inequality: What It Is and Why It Matters', DESA Working Paper No. 26, United Nations Department of Social and Economic Affairs, New York, USA.

Parfit, D. (1997),'Equality and Priority', *Ratio (new series)* 10(3): 202-21.

Pogge, T.W. (2003), '"Assisting" the Global Poor', available at http://www.etikk.no/globaljustice/papers/GJ2003_Thomas_Pogge_Assisting_the_Global_Poor.DOC (accessed on 7 April 2008).

Reddy, S.G. (2007), 'International Debt: The Constructive Implications of Some Moral Mathematics', *Ethics and International Affairs*, 21(1): 33–48.

Subramanian, S. (2003), 'Aspects of Global Deprivation and Disparity: A Child's Guide to Some Simple-Minded Arithmetic', in F. Carlucci and F. Marzano (eds), *Poverty, Growth and Welfare in the World Economy in the 21st Century*. Bern: Peter Lang.

———. (2006), 'Poverty Measures and Anti-Poverty Policy under an Egalitarian Constraint', in S. Subramanian, *Rights, Deprivation, and Disparity: Essays in Concepts and Measurement*. New Delhi: Oxford University Press.

———. (2007), 'International Aid in Light of Global Poverty and Inequality', UNU-WIDER Research Paper No. 2007/31, Helsinki.

Timmermann, J. (2004), 'The Individualist Lottery: How People Count, but Not Their Numbers', *Analysis*, 64: 106–12.

Domestic Deprivation and Disparity

Table 2.2 continued

3

The Status of the Child in India*

Introduction

This is not a learned paper. It will be largely bereft of such things as tables, equations, charts, nuanced analysis, and other allied appurtenances of scholarly enquiry (even if footnotes and references should occasionally and unavoidably find their way in). Furthermore, the essay will be entirely innocent of startling insights and revelatory findings. What it will be, for the most part, is a re-telling of things we are all already familiar with, but in a form which, one hopes, will have the merit of presenting facts and issues after a more or less systematic and orderly fashion. This seems to me to be the right approach to adopt in what, to remind ourselves, is a keynote address, and not a paper destined for an academic journal. But even setting this fact aside, it is my belief that there is no harm in, and every advantage to, reviewing and reiterating what all of us—academics, or bureaucrats, or policy-makers, or involved citizens—know to be the truth. This is because we often tend to take what we know for granted: familiarity breeds forgetfulness. At other times, knowledge fails to breed acknowledgement, so that we fail to act on what we know. For all these reasons, this will be

* An abbreviated version of this essay was presented as a key-note address at a workshop organized by UNICEF in Chennai in 2002.

a simple and essentially modest effort aimed at providing an organized repetition of known facts. The cards are on the table, and no apologies, I hope you will agree, are in order.

Background: India's Social Sector Performance

Before we undertake a more particular examination of the status of the child in India, it is useful to try and locate that exercise in a broader perspective of how India has been doing on the social sector front. With this in mind I provide, in what follows, a (necessarily) rapid and cursory sketch of some aspects of 'illfare' in India (for which I draw heavily on Subramanian, 2000).

Consider, first, the country's track record in the matter of *income poverty*. India plays host to the largest population of poor persons in the world, adding up to something like 325 millions. After achieving independence in 1947, the country's major preoccupation—in principle even if not necessarily in fact—has been with combating poverty. India has an impressive time-series data base on the distribution of consumption expenditure, thanks to the efforts of the Central Statistical Organization and its various rounds of national sample surveys. The official poverty line employed, in conformity with a methodology advanced by the Union Planning Commission, is based on the level of consumption expenditure corresponding to the achievement of a specified calorific norm of nutritional intake. The headcount index of poverty, in relation to such a poverty line, rose through the 1950s and 1960s, and began declining in the 1970s and then more rapidly in the 1980s, so that it was only towards the beginning of the 1980s that the poverty ratio was restored to its levels of the early 1960s. As far as the 1990s are concerned, Gaurav Datt's (1999) statistical analysis suggests that while urban poverty has declined in the period 1991–97, the trend of declining rural poverty of the 1980s would appear to have been arrested in the post-reform period. Indeed, according to his estimates, the average rural headcount ratio for the (immediately pre-reform) period July 1989–June 1991, at 35.4 per cent, was a little lower than the average headcount ratio for the (post-reform) period July 1995–December 1997, at 36.5 per cent. Apart from an accentuation of intersectoral (rural–urban) inequality in living standards, the absence of any gain on the rural poverty front is a matter of concern in the context of the country's 'reform' experience.

Throughout the post-independence period, inequality in the distribution of consumption expenditure has been high, as reflected in a Gini coefficient (which is the economist's favourite summary measure of inequality) of 0.3 or more. There have also been pronounced inequalities in the distribution of both land and non-land assets, with Gini coefficients of inter-household inequality easily clearing a value of 0.6.

Moving away from income-related indicators to an assessment of more direct functionings in various dimensions, India's track record, notwithstanding the initial infirmities imposed upon it by its colonial inheritance, has been disappointing. In the matter of literacy, for example, despite constitutional aspirations for the provision of universal mandatory primary education for all children below the age of 14 years within the first 10 years of independence, adult literates in the census of India 2001 accounted for less than two-thirds of the adult population. In the matter of demographic indicators, information in the UNDP's *HDR*, 1999, suggests that the expectation of life at birth in India in 1997 was 62.6 years, lower than in both China (69.8 years) and Sri Lanka (73.1 years). Over 1990–97 (again see HDR 1999), the proportion of India's population without access to safe water was 19 per cent, while 71 per cent lacked access to sanitation. A quarter of the population did not have access to health services. These input failures are reflected in corresponding outcome failures: SWC 1999 data suggest that India's crude death rate in 1997 was 9 per 1,000 population (China: 7 per 1,000 and Sri Lanka: 6 per 1,000), while the infant mortality rate was 71 per 1,000 live births (China: 38 and Sri Lanka: 17). An aspect of vital demographic significance is the reproductive burden borne by women, one indicator of which is the total fertility rate (TFR). At 3.1 in 1997, the TFR in India was still high, and scarcely suggestive of an accomplished demographic transition; data from SWC 1999 indicate the vastly greater successes of China and Sri Lanka in this regard, with TFR figures of 1.8 and 2.1, respectively. As Partha Dasgupta (1993) has pointed out, fertility decisions are often dictated by the necessity of employing children as 'producer goods' in an environment where firewood and potable water require arduous gathering and fetching. Inadequate access to health services and to literacy enhances infant mortality which in turn promotes higher levels of fertility; likewise, inadequate access to elementary infrastructural resources of energy and drinking water promotes both excess fertility and environmental degradation which latter, in turn, provokes further excess fertility in a vicious circle.

Whether we speak of income poverty or illiteracy or under-nutrition or lack of access to health services or infant mortality, there are pronounced and systematic biases, within a generalized environment of deprivation, against particular, identifiable groups of the population, classified on the basis of sector of origin, caste, occupation, and gender. This becomes starkly manifest when one looks at the capability status (or rather lack of it) of an average rural, landless, scheduled caste, and female person.

By way of a quick summary of a quick summary, India's track record of achievement on the social sector front is such that it would be churlish to deny evidence of secular improvement over the long haul. Having said this, it is also difficult to deny that the nature of progress has been a gradual transition from the terrible to the merely awful. As regrettable as it is inevitable, the same must be expected to hold true for the status of the child in India, to a consideration of which I now turn.

Nutritional, Health, and Educational Status of the Child

According to data provided in SWC 1999, one-third of all infants in India, over the period 1990–97, were low (i.e., less than 2.5 kg) birthweight babies, which is nearly twice the proportion for the world as a whole (17 per cent), contrasts very poorly with the corresponding statistics for China (9 per cent), and poorly enough with those for Sri Lanka (25 per cent) or Mozambique (20 per cent). According to the same data source, and over the same period, the proportion of under-fives that were moderately and severely underweight (i.e., below median weight for age less two standard deviations of the reference population) was 53 per cent for India, with corresponding figures of 16 per cent for China and 34 per cent for Sri Lanka; in a similar pattern of contrast that shows India in a relatively unfavourable light, the proportion of under-fives that were moderately and severely stunted (i.e., below median height for age less two standard deviations of the reference population) was 52 per cent in India, 34 per cent in China, and 14 per cent in Sri Lanka. All of this points to a considerable incidence of chronic undernourishment of the child in India, despite such gains as have undoubtedly been secured through Noon Meal Schemes and similar feeding programmes in schools. An elementary indicator of access to a basic health service is the extent of 'ORT use', defined in SWC 1999 as the percentage of all cases of diarrhoea in under-fives treated with oral rehydration salts and/or recommended home fluids. For the period 1990–97, the extent of ORT use in India was 67 per cent, still 6 percentage points behind the figure for the world as a whole. The picture of undernutrition and ill health is completed, in an unhappy triad, by statistics on educational deprivation: the percentage of primary school entrants that made it to grade 5 in India, over the period 1990–95, was 62 per cent, with corresponding figures for China, Sri Lanka, and the world, of 92 per cent, 98 per cent, and 78 per cent, respectively. High dropout ratios at such an elementary stage of schooling must be expected to be accompanied by high rates of child labour (on which more later).

Infant and Child Mortality

Before considering the statistics on infant and child mortality, it is instructive to take a quick look at the age structure of the population, which is an aspect of demography that is not only of independent interest, but also has some implications for an assessment of the well-being of children. (I owe the following discussion entirely to my colleague D. Jayaraj.) It has been observed by other commentators that the age structure of the Indian population now is not vastly different from what it was at the turn of the (preceding) century. Are we to infer then that none of the factors which influence the age structure of a population has changed over the last century? Before addressing this question, let us first take a look at the inter-temporal picture of the Indian population's age structure. As I have just indicated, the 1901 and 1991 age structures of the Indian population look pretty similar. However, this conceals changes that have occurred along the way. Specifically, if we compare the 1901 and 1961 populations, we find that the 'younger' cohorts account for a larger share of the population in 1961 than in 1901, while if we compare the 1961 and 1991 populations, we find that the 'younger' cohorts account for a smaller proportion of the population in 1991 than in 1961. To state the matter grossly, the period 1901–61 could be characterized as one of rising birth rates, and the period 1961–91 as one of declining birth, death, and infant mortality rates. The age structures in 1901 and 1991 may be similar, but a given symptom is associated with vastly different causations: in 1901, compared with 1991, the share of infant deaths in all deaths was higher and the longevity of the population was smaller. The process of development must be acknowledged to have had some beneficent effects.

This last proposition is reflected quite clearly in data (from the Sample Registration System) on infant mortality, which is a crucial indicator of a population's well-being, over the 15-year period from 1978 to 1992, when the number of infant deaths per 1,000 live births registered a more or less continuous decline from 126 to 79. The *trend* is encouraging, but the absolute magnitudes are not. Over this same period, mortality differentials as between females and males generally improved in favour of the former (which it is a pity to treat as a remarkable phenomenon, given that female infants are known to have a 'natural', 'biological' edge over male infants). In general, however, the unflattering fact of high prevalent rates of infant mortality in India is rendered even worse when we take an account of regional, caste, sector of origin, and gender-based disparities. Thus, for example, Majumdar and Subramanian (2001) report estimates for 1984 which indicate that while the infant mortality rate for the urban non-scheduled caste and tribe population in Kerala was 26.8, the corresponding figure for the rural scheduled caste and tribe population in Uttar Pradesh was as high as 187.9.

Elementary initiatives in development can secure large reductions in the tragedy of infant mortality: as Nagaraj (1992) has pointed out, there are considerable returns to be had from anti-tetanus vaccination for expectant mothers, provision of clean drinking water, and oral rehydration—not to mention an accelerated impetus to female literacy.

Where does India stand with respect to child mortality (defined as the number of under-fives deaths in the reference year for every 1,000 live births)? According to data provided for 1997 in SWC 1999, India's child mortality rate was 108, which compares poorly with the global average of 85. It may be added here that the global picture is characterized by an enormous degree of cross-country disparity. The child mortality figure ranges from 4 per 1,000 live births for the Scandinavian countries to a shocking 320 per 1,000 live births for Niger and 316 for Sierra Leone. Grouped data bring out the disparities sharply. Sub-Saharan Africa, with an under-5 mortality rate of 169, exceeds the record (81) of its nearest 'competitor', Asia and the Pacific, by a factor of more than 200 per cent; the latter, in turn, together with the Arab states, exceeds the child mortality rate (41) of Latin America and the Caribbean (LAC) by a factor again of around 200 per cent; while the LAC countries themselves exceed the child mortality rate for the industrialized countries (6.7) by a factor of 612 per cent. Under-five mortality for Sub-Saharan Africa exceeds that in the industrialized countries by a factor greater than 2,500 per cent. Such disparities are seriously gross. The predicament of Indian or African children only acquires an added bitter twist when it is located in its global context.

Gender Discrimination: Sex-selective Infanticide and Foeticide

An extreme form of discrimination against the girl child (respectively, girl child-to-be), which constitutes a particularly horrific aspect of the general status of the child in India, is manifested in the act of female infanticide (respectively, female foeticide). While female infanticide has been known to be prevalent in parts of India in pre-colonial times, there has been a resurgence of the practice over the last couple of decades, notably in (selected regions of) the states of Haryana, Punjab, Rajasthan, Uttar Pradesh, Gujarat, Madhya Pradesh, and Tamil Nadu (Chunkath and Athreya, 1997). The first systematic account of the practice, as it has manifested itself in Tamil Nadu, is available in the work of Chunkath and Athreya (1997). Employing information available in Public Health Centre records, a statewide sample survey undertaken by the department of public health, and field investigations, the authors present a statistical picture of the incidence of female infanticide in Tamil Nadu which strongly suggests a widespread prevalence of the practice in the districts of Dharmapuri, Salem, Dindigul, and Madurai. Apart from sexist and patriarchal ideology which breeds generalized son-preference, there would also appear to be a material basis to the sudden spurt of female infanticide: namely, the desire to avoid the costs of ritual expenditures on girls which the relatively 'backward' castes have, in a process of 'sanskritization', increasingly felt compelled to see as part of their socially necessary expenditure, in emulation of the 'higher' castes' practices in this regard.

With the availability of technologies for sex detection *in utero*, we are also witness to an aspect of 'gender-cleansing' (Harriss-White, 1999) which does not have to wait for the child to be born: termination of pregnancy upon determination of the sex of the foetus is an option that is being increasingly resorted to by the relatively more affluent classes of society. Since female foeticide is, by its nature, both criminal and clandestine, it is difficult to have an assessment of precisely how widespread the practice is. Quite independently of the extent of its spread, it is an abhorrent practice, and constitutes one of the most dismal aspects of the Indian child's predicament today.

A related issue, concerning the weight of women in a population, deserves consideration in this context. It is widely held that the sex ratio of a population (defined as the number of females per 1,000 males) is a significant indicator of the relative well-being of women in a society. It is also widely known that the sex ratio of the Indian population has displayed a more or less continuous decline over the last century. In principle, both female infanticide and female foeticide could contribute to the lowness and declining trend of the sex ratio. However, recent trends of relatively female-favourable sex ratios of infant mortality suggest that sex-selective infanticide has probably not contributed significantly to the declining overall sex ratio. Further, overall relative female survival advantage has, in recent decades, been improving. It is now believed by some demographers (see Krishnaji [2000] for a review) that over the last decade and more, declines in the *sex ratio at birth* (SRB), caused by an increasing incidence of sex-selective foeticide, have probably contributed much to the decline in the overall sex ratio of the population.

As a mono-causal explanation of the declining sex ratio of the population, it is possible that the phenomenon of female foeticide is perhaps being made to bear too heavy a burden. Given the relatively high costs of sex-detection and the relatively restricted access to reliable technology needed for it, foeticide is (fortunately) probably nowhere near as widespread as it would need to be in order to account substantially for a decline in the overall sex ratio. Further, work by Jayaraj (2001) and on-going research by Jayaraj and Subramanian suggest that the SRB has had a fairly long history of decline in India, predating the appearance of sex detection technologies in the country. What, then, might cause a decline in the SRB? Jayaraj (2001) hypothesizes that given (a) that males greatly preponderate over females at conception and (b) that the male embryo is less hardy than the female, a sex-neutral reduction in the rate of foetal loss (spontaneous abortions and still births) must be expected to lower the SRB. Foetal loss, in turn, is postulated to be a declining function of the mother's nutritional status. Over the long haul, if there have been improvements in the economic status of the family, average food intake by women, access to health care facilities, age at marriage, and the reproductive burden of women, then foetal loss—and therefore the SRB (and therefore, other things equal, the overall sex ratio of the population)—might be expected to decline. There is reason to believe that the process of development, restricted in pace and gender-wise lopsided though it has been, has nevertheless improved the well-being status of the Indian woman over time, with obvious implications for the well-being of her children, too. I bring up this issue in order to urge the cautionary note that an excessive invocation of the profoundly distressing practice of female foeticide, *in the context of explaining the declining trend of the overall sex ratio of the population*, could have the unfortunate consequence of distracting attention from the centrally important role which the processes of development have to play in the link connecting the welfare of the woman with the welfare of the child. The centrality of developmental processes in a child's well-being status is again sharply brought out in a consideration of the phenomenon of child labour, to which I now turn.

Child Labour

Much has been written, and much is known, about the phenomenon of child labour in India. In what follows, I shall draw heavily on a study by Jayaraj and Subramanian (1999) on Tamil Nadu, which perhaps has certain general implications for tendencies elsewhere too. Official sources of data adopt a narrow, conservative view of child labour: in terms of this 'restrictive' definition, a child labourer is taken to be a child who is engaged in 'gainful' employment, which leaves out of the count children who are not gainfully employed, but are not in school attendance either — children, that is, who may be engaged in unpaid domestic work or in production-related activities the output of which is not marketed. Even under the conservative, 'restricted' definition, the magnitude of child labour in Tamil Nadu, as revealed by N(ational) S(ample) S(urvey) data for 1987–89, was large, at 11 per every 1,000 children. The count becomes even more disturbingly large when we resort to the 'liberal' definition: going by Census 1981 (respectively, NSS, 1983) figures, the number of child workers per 1,000 is over 40 (respectively, 33). These figures suggest that the very large presence of orderly, systematic child labour and child illiteracy, together with their thorough dispersal across space, has rendered the phenomenon of child labour an unremarkable, everyday occurrence: its (shocking) neglect, contrasted with the (commendable, even if oftentimes tokenistic) attention that has been paid to particular forms of child labour in particular industries (matchworks, *bidi*-manufacturing), mirrors the perceptual divide that presides over the large-scale incidence of chronic undernutrition on the one hand, and its intensification, on the other, into starvation under conditions of famine (Sen, 1981).

An analysis of the occupation-wise contribution to overall child-labour intensity (under the 'restrictive' definition) suggests that the occupations significantly associated with the employment of child labour are also the occupations characterized by a relatively high order of casualization of the workforce, a high level of illiteracy among workers and depressed levels of wages and skill-formation. The distribution of those children who are neither 'gainfully employed' nor in school, according to their main activity, is suggestive of a strong gender bias (against girls) in the matter of (a) perceptions relating to age and disability as being the reason for failing to be in school and (b) the allocation of onerous household duties and domestic chores between the sexes: the marginalization of a woman's work, in more senses than one, clearly begins at an early age, and is aided both by low levels of enrolment into and high levels of dropping out of the school system. An examination of the distribution of child labour across well-defined socio-economic groups indicates that a disproportionate burden of the overheads of child labour is borne by girls relative to boys; by children of rural origin relative to those of urban origin and by scheduled caste/scheduled tribe (SC/ST) children relative to non-SC/T children. It is bad enough that (under the 'liberal' definition, based on 1981 Census data) the work participation rate of urban, non-SC/T boys, is of the high order of 24 per cent, but this pales into insignificance when set against the corresponding figure for rural SC/T girls which is in the region of 70 per cent! In this, as in other dimensions of deprivation in India, a concern over what is bad is swiftly deflected by a discovery of something even worse.

Child labour is found (unsurprisingly) to be strongly correlated with deprivation and capability failure. For the rural areas of the districts of Tamil Nadu, based on 1981 Census data, Jayaraj and

Subramanian (1999) have computed an aggregate generalized headcount index H of deprivation that measures the proportion of individual instances of failure to have access to certain very basic capabilities to function in the dimensions of literacy, health, drinking water, mobility and shelter. The district-wise rural work participation rates for 1981 are found to be strongly and significantly positively correlated with the district-wise measures of H. Child labour clearly flourishes in an environment of generalized deprivation.

This brings one back to the (admittedly commonplace, but hard-to-deny) theme of the centrality of development in the scheme of things. Many years ago, the demographer Robert Cassen (1978) observed that anything that needs doing from a population point of view needs doing anyway. In a similar vein, it appears to be fair to suggest that anything that needs doing from the perspective of the child's interest needs doing anyway. But are the international and national environments in which we function today such as to reflect an adequate appreciation of these truisms? Distressingly not, as the discussion below suggests.

The Global Environment

It has been noted in Section 6 that, in the matter of child mortality, the global picture is characterized by massive disparities in cross-country performance. This is unhappily true for several development indicators, including those relating to knowledge, longevity and income. A perusal of the UNDP's published statistics on the 'Human Development Indicator', available in successive rounds of the *HDR* over the decade of the 1990s, makes for depressing reading: inter-country disparities have been steadily increasing over time, accentuating over and over again the divide between the North and the South—these matters have been dealt with at some length in Chapter 1.

The conditionalities imposed by multilateral lending agencies seek to reduce the fiscal deficit of a developing country, which for the most part translates to cutting down on already small levels of social sector spending. Much effort is expended by the industrialized countries in purportedly defending the rights of the Third World child, by placing trade sanctions on products entailing the use of child labour. This, for the most part, is thinly disguised protectionism. A more credible statement of benign intent would consist in deferring to the Pearson Committee's (1969) recommendation that developed countries should allocate a small proportion (just 0.7 per cent, as it happens) of their GNP to international aid: any conditionality that requires at least 50 per cent of this aid to be spent by the recipient country on well-defined developmental programmes targeted at women and children would be more than welcome. One recognizes, though, that this is not much more than a counsel of perfection.

The Domestic Environment

As we have repeatedly seen, any improvement in the sad status of the average Indian child would call for some seriousness in addressing the developmental needs of the country. In this context, it has to be admitted that state policy, on the whole, has been disappointing and has fallen considerably short of what might have been achieved. While social security provisions in the organized sector are limited enough, they are cripplingly inadequate for the bulk of the population constituting the unorganized sector. At a general level, social sector spending by the state has been grossly suboptimal in the country. Furthermore, the state has failed to engage in any seriously or significantly redistributivist programme as a means to combating deprivation (as reflected in its feeble efforts at land reform or agricultural sector taxation). Following on the severe balance of payments crisis that occurred in 1990, India had to resort to large-scale borrowing from the International Monetary Fund; and partly under the compulsions of borrowing conditionalities which require macroeconomic stabilization through curtailment of the fiscal deficit, there have been further restrictions on an already low level of public expenditure on both the social sector and capital formation. In recent times, the public distribution system (PDS) has come under considerable pressure: while the official poverty lines employed are not much more than destitution lines, the coverage of the PDS has been shrunk to keep those above the poverty line out of the ambit of its provision of food and other essential commodities, whereas the prices for those below the poverty line have been raised. Worst of all, we are now witness to large numbers of the poor of this country having to suffer hunger when the state's storehouses are overflowing with foodgrains and the state's spokesmen are busy attributing death to causes other than starvation.

One of the most pernicious symptoms of failure in governance has to do with corruption. A major aspect of corruption on the part of the Indian public has been the failure to declare income and wealth; and a major aspect of public sector corruption has been the failure to detect and punish tax evasion. Subramanian and Harriss-White (1999) provide an elementary example of the implications of such permissive non-compliance for poverty in the country. They suggest that the returns from just a small segment of 'underground' wealth, held in the form of smuggled gold over the 5-year period 1990–95, should suffice to eliminate a large part of the country's aggregate poverty deficit. At a broad level, one has to conclude that the prospects of sensitive state attention to the problems of the deprived are becoming increasingly attenuated in a time of globalization. This is as much because of the macroeconomic compulsions, in terms of prioritization of concerns, to which a poor country is subjected by globalization, as because of the very 'culture' of globalization, with its emphasis on incentives and efficiency, and its soft-pedalling of issues concerned with social obligation and onus.

Concluding Remarks

I have made an effort to present some features of the status of the child in India, in terms of a set of rather elementary indicators of well-being. While there have been over-time improvements in these indicators, the present level of overall achievement is disappointing, in both absolute and relative (that is, vis-à-vis comparably income-poor countries) senses. It has been repeatedly stressed in the course of this address that further urgently needed improvements in the status of the child would have to be predicated on an accelerated rate of state intervention in developmental processes, conceived of in terms of what Amartya Sen refers to as *basic capabilities*. Additionally, development must also be specifically targeted to the needs of women and children. For the former, this would entail measures aimed at securing both negative and positive freedoms: protection from discrimination, both in domestic and work settings, and provision of enabling capabilities, particularly in the realms of literacy and reproductive health. Where the child is concerned, there is much that still needs to be done in the matter of provisioning relating to schools, creches, immunization programmes and supplementary nutrition, apart from legal and social reforms in the context of adoption, child abuse and child labour.

All of this requires resources. It is my contention that the problem of resource constraints can be, and frequently is, exaggerated. Fairly small redistributivist measures (for example, a 'poverty surcharge' on the incomes of the relatively affluent); a minimally serious engagement with recovering a small share of the 'underground' economy; some tightening-up with respect to wasteful and negligent public spending (what in polite officialese is described as 'leakage'); and a certain reigning-in of the unbridled corruption that now marks much of political and government practice: these efforts should release resources that can make a significant difference to the quality of our children's lives. The participation of citizens, individually and collectively, in this effort hardly needs to be underlined. However, impatience with the failures of the state, together with a failure to appreciate the benefits of state-sponsored development initiatives, has increasingly been a part of the discourse of both the politically 'right' and the politically 'radical' constituencies of society. As a consequence, there have been increasingly articulated demands to leave the processes of development to be largely worked out either by the 'market' or by the 'community'. Whether or not this is intended, an unwelcome outcome of these positions has been to simply let the state off the hook. I would be inclined to put the state, and its accountability for development in general and our children in particular, back on the agendum.

And while we are about this task, and since a question of the children of our country is involved, I would like to submit that, from somewhere, we should also try and find a little compassion to help us on our way.

References

Cassen, R. (1978), *India: Population, Economy, Society*. London: Macmillan.

Chunkath, S.R. and V.B. Athreya. (1997), 'Female Infanticide in Tamilnadu: Some Evidence', *Economic and Political Weekly*, 32(17): 22–9.

Dasgupta, P.S. (1993), *An Inquiry into Well-being and Destitution*. Oxford: Clarendon Press.

Datt, G. (1999), 'Has Poverty Declined Since Economic Reforms? Statistical Data Analysis', *Economic and Political Weekly*, 34(50): 3516–8.

Harriss-White, B. (1999), 'Gender Cleansing: The Paradox of Development and Deteriorating Female Life Chances in Tamilnadu', in R. Sunder Rajan (ed.), *Signposts: Gender Issues in Post-Independence India*. New Delhi: Kali for Women.

Jayaraj, D. (2001), 'The Sex Ratio at Birth and its Determinants: An Exploratory Analysis', *mimeo*, Madras Institute of Development Studies.

Jayaraj, D. and S. Subramanian. (1999), 'Child Labour in Tamilnadu: A Preliminary Account of its Nature, Extent and Distribution', *mimeo*, Madras Institute of Development Studies, forthcoming in *Economic and Political Weekly*. (Subsequently published in *Economic and Political Weekly*, 37(10): 941–54.)

Krishnaji, N. (2000), 'Trends in Sex Ratio: A Review in Tribute to Asok Mitra', *Economic and Political Weekly*, 35(14): 1161–3.

Majumdar, M. and S. Subramanian. (2001), 'Capability Failure and Group Disparities: Some Evidence from India for the 1980s', *Journal of Development Studies*, 37(5): 104–40.

Nagaraj, K. (1992), 'Infant Mortality in Tamilnadu', in S. Subramanian (ed.), *Themes in Development Economics: Essays in Honour of Malcolm Adiseshiah*. New Delhi: Oxford University Press.

Sen, A. (1981), *Poverty and Famines: An Essay on Entitlement and Deprivation*. New Delhi: Oxford University Press.

Subramanian, S. (2000), *Aspects of Global Deprivation and Disparity: A Child's Guide to Some Simple-minded Arithmetic*, *mimeo*, Madras Institute of Development Studies: S. Guhan Memorial Series Monograph No. 2.

Subramanian, S. and B. Harriss-White. (1999), 'Introduction', in B. Harriss-White and S. Subramanian (eds), *Illfare in India: Essays in Honour of S. Guhan*. New Delhi: SAGE Publications.

4

Human Development and Human Rights*

*

Three useful analytical categories in terms of which the subject of 'socio-economic development and human rights' can be appraised are those of *positive freedom, negative freedom,* and *discrimination*.

The notion of 'positive freedom' is best captured in what Amartya Sen has referred to as the *capability to function*. The reference here is to the ability which human beings have to lead the 'good life', and the practical question is one of the power which individuals enjoy, or which they are enabled by society to acquire, in order to achieve various valued human 'functionings', a functioning being what Sen again calls 'a state of being or doing'. An indicative and elementary list of freedoms which a well-ordered society might be expected to guarantee for its citizens would be reflected in the satisfaction of certain 'positive rights', such as

the right not to be hungry;
the right to a reasonably long and healthy life;

* Text of a talk delivered at Holy Cross College, Tiruchirapalli, in February 2004. Large parts of this essay were subsequently employed in the author's entry on 'Poverty' in Kaushik Basu (ed.) (2007), *Oxford Companion to Economics in India*. New Delhi: Oxford University Press.

the right to livelihood;
the right to a decent standard of living;
the right to shelter and clothing;
the right to knowledge;
the right to mobility;
the right not to be systematically disadvantaged by, and vulnerable to, Acts of God;
and so on

The notion of 'negative freedom' is captured by what one might call 'libertarianism', namely the acknowledgement that each individual is entitled to a 'personal protected sphere', as John Stuart Mill called it, such that within her or his protected sphere, the individual is in no way subjected to any let or hindrance in the pursuit of her or his desired goals. Freedom of conscience, of speech, of religious conviction, of political affiliation and of association—these are examples of libertarian human rights. While positive freedom is concerned with 'enablement', negative freedom is concerned with 'absence of restraint'.

If the extent to which positive and negative freedoms are secured for the citizens of a society constitutes an important index of that society's well-being and development, of comparable concern should be the *equitableness* with which the fulfilment of these rights is distributed across the population. A society guilty of discriminatory practice is one which presides over an inequitable distribution of rights across individuals on the strength of their group affiliation—where the grouping in question corresponds to some partitioning of the population on the basis, by way of example, of caste or religion or gender or age or geographical sector of origin. When one speaks of non-discrimination, the concern is with substantive, as opposed to merely formal, equality: the former is concerned with 'the right to treatment as an equal', namely, the 'right to be treated with the same respect and concern as anyone else', whereas the latter is concerned with 'the right to equal treatment', namely, 'the right to an equal distribution of the burdens and benefits of society'. The right to treatment as an equal, it may be held, is primary; the right to equal treatment is derivative, and contingent on the satisfaction of the more basic right to equality, interpreted as the right to treatment as an equal. These distinctions and priorities are due to the philosopher and scholar of jurisprudence, Ronald Dworkin; and they lie at the heart of the case in favour of 'compensatory discrimination' or 'affirmative action'.

*

How has India fared with respect to securing any large measure of positive freedoms for the bulk of its citizens? I shall not bore you with statistics, but shall take you on a swift and selective qualitative survey of the record. As Amartya Sen has pointed out, there has been no large-scale famine in independent India, unlike in colonial India, whereas, on the other hand, there is a great deal of persistent and endemic hunger in the country: undernourishment is still an integral aspect of the socio-economic profile of India's population. The incidence of low birth-weight babies, and of stunting and wasting among children, is still disquietingly large in comparison with the record of neighbouring countries such as China and Sri Lanka. Nor is the country—especially in parts of it like Orissa— exempt from a periodic occurrence of starvation deaths, which is particularly unacceptable in a time of self-sufficiency (in terms of the availability of foodgrains on a *per caput* basis) and of bursting public granaries. The expectation of life at birth has increased from 23 at the beginning of the preceding century to a little over 60 at the beginning of this century, and yet lags behind the Chinese and Sri Lankan figures. The trend in infant mortality is a definitely declining one, but its absolute levels are still such as to cause anxiety. In terms of guarding against child morbidity and mortality through elementary precautions such as oral re-hydration therapy, there have been secular improvements, but at a pace so retarded as to cause India to still lag behind the global average performance. Unemployment, which is intimately linked with poverty, continues to remain a major block to socio-economic development: joblessness, intermittency, seasonality, and sporadicity of employment, retarded rates of skill-learning and segmentation of the labour market, casualization of the labour force and depressed wage rates are not ideal guarantors of the right to livelihood. Income poverty levels, in terms of the headcount ratio and other more sophisticated measures of poverty, are reported to have registered a steady decline from towards the end of the 1970s to the present. One wonders though what the statistics would look like if one were to readjust the poverty line to reflect possible changes in needs, priorities and expectations. In any event, the aggregate headcount should also be expected to matter in the scheme of things: with about 300 million poor persons in the country today, the record is scarcely better than what it was 40 years ago; and India has the dubious distinction of being the largest contributing country to the world's poor. Further, the country is far removed from a state where the absence of homelessness is a universal reality; and where housing is available, it is often of the semi-*pucca* or *kutcha* variety. While literacy levels have gradually increased over time, with about two-thirds of the population now reported to be literate, this still leaves behind a third of a vast population unable to read or write a short statement on their everyday life. Apart from the intrinsic importance of the right to knowledge, literacy has also been found to have many instrumental advantages, such as in being associated with declines in fertility, which can only be for the good in the context of population stabilization. The public provisioning of aids to mobility— railways, roadways, transport vehicles and subsidized travel—has improved over time, but shows signs of slackening in an era of deregulation and privatization. Despite repeated encounters with the forces of nature, identifiable sections of the population in identifiable parts of the country continue to be predictably vulnerable to natural disasters such as floods, cyclones and droughts. Briefly, a charitable assessment of India's track record in the matter of positive freedoms would be: 'not bad;' but not bad only in relation to historically very high levels of illfare. It is, unhappily, not good— either in relation to the country's own potential or in relation to the record of other comparably poor countries. I must emphasize that this diagnosis of inadequate state success is not intended to seek a replacement of the state by the market or civil society, but rather to seek enhanced levels of public pressure on the state for significantly better delivery and accountability.

*

What can one say of India's record in the sphere of securing negative freedoms for its citizens? How unfettered a citizen is is reflected in the extent of protection of her or his legal entitlements. The measure of liberty available is, therefore, a function of (a) the ambit of legal protection available, and (b) the quality of governance that mediates the implementation of the provisions of the law. In India, there is good, bad and indifferent law, but a substantial part of it is legislation aimed at protecting individual liberties, which holds out promise for development through the exercise of libertarian rights. The hiatus between good law and effective implementation is, however, vast.

At the executive level, there is far too much corruption—in a nexus among politicians, bureaucrats and organized crime—to foster any large expectation of socio-economic development through the safeguarding of individual liberties. There are two issues to be considered here: first, the prospect of securing the positive freedoms of the disadvantaged sections of society is often contingent on limiting the negative freedoms of the advantaged sections of society and second, the positive freedoms of the latter class are often better secured simply because of both the immunity and influence enjoyed by it as a consequence of its superior status in respect of negative freedoms. Poor socio-economic development must be expected to be an outcome of a sociopolitical system which is largely unprepared to disturb the settled weight of vested interests in a deeply stratified society. For example, India's poor record of land redistribution is a reflection of far greater concern for the negative right of private property for the few than for the positive right of a minimally decent standard of living for the many. In a related context, budgetary resources for securing an improved quality of life for the many are severely compromised by the inability or unwillingness to deal effectively with the crime of undeclared wealth and incomes perpetrated by the few.

The consequences of such a regime of scant general regard for personal liberties, and the extension of liberties beyond permissible bounds to license for a few, are there for all to see and for most to suffer. It is no surprise that, in the reckoning of agencies like Transparency International, India should occupy a comfortable position in the upper 80th percentile of the corrupt nations of the world. Clearly, there is not much that can be said for the protection of negative freedoms in an environment which is mediated as much as ours is by routine, everyday corruption, as manifested, say, in land evictions, rapes, riots, fraud, bribery, and scams of every conceivable description. Add the phenomenon of judicial delays, and the increasing wearing away of the autonomy of investigating, enforcement, and judicial agencies from political interference, not to mention growing political intolerance of the freedom of the press, and the picture is in no way improved. The great promise of democracy which India held out to the rest of the world in 1947 has degenerated over the years into securing votes through the currency of money and muscle, and to 'collective' decision-making through the brute force of majoritarianism. The picture is scarcely pretty, but as my late friend and colleague S. Guhan has said: '[P]essimism, like optimism, must be sober.' Things might have been so much worse without a (even if qualifiedly) free press and parliamentary democracy.

*

What has India's record on the front of 'discrimination' been? Honesty must compel the conclusion that here, more than anywhere else, the country's experience of socio-economic achievement has been acutely shameful. Consider the distribution of positive freedoms across well-defined social groupings, effected on the basis of caste, sector of origin and gender, for instance. Whether we speak of hunger or health or mobility or knowledge or poverty, the SCs and STs are systematically and significantly worse off than the rest; people of rural origin are worse off than those of urban origin; and females are worse off than males. The picture is a faithful reflection of the group-wise distribution of personal liberties. Dalits are still subjected to caste atrocities; religious minorities are the victims of state-abetted genocide; women are discriminated against in the intra-family distribution of resources, in the intra-family allocation of work burdens, in the acquisition and utilization of skills in the labour market, in the payment of wages, and in the display of respect towards their privacy and their bodies, as reflected in the phenomena of rape, forced prostitution, dowry deaths, female infanticide and foeticide, and ritual burning on the funeral pyres of their husbands. If one accepts the philosopher John Rawls' criterion of reckoning the welfare of a society in terms of the welfare of its most deprived member, then India's socio-economic achievement, as crystallized in the predicament of a poor, illiterate, rural, SC woman, is a thing of shame.

*

Let me conclude. It cannot have escaped anyone's attention that the preceding assessment of India's socio-economic development, as reckoned through its track record in the matter of human rights, in terms of the categories of positive and negative freedoms and the extent of group-wise discrimination in their distribution, has been less than flattering. Such criticism, in the light of an immoderate and illiberal 'nationalism' as is increasingly being projected as the need of the hour, must meet with disapproval. It is useful, here, to invoke a distinction which the poet Nissim Ezekiel once made: that between criticism emanating from petulance, and criticism emanating from involvement. Nobody who cares for India and the country's socio-economic development through the fulfilment of human rights can be accused of wanting in involvement, nor be expected to be other than severely critical. Patriotism is not achieved by edgy defensiveness, nor by rationalizing our poor socio-economic indicators by pointing to Sierra Leone or Bangladesh; our caste-discrimination by pointing to the erstwhile apartheid regime in South Africa; our abuse of human rights by pointing to Rwanda; our levels of corruption by pointing to Nigeria; and our treatment of our women by pointing to Afghanistan. A proper love of country, I would argue, demands that we look above and within ourselves for the setting of standards, while reaching out a hand in friendship to those that might not have caught up with us. 'India Shining', I am sure, is something we all aspire to. The promise of socio-economic development through a proper regard for human rights is an exacting one. It calls, I would submit, for effort that is deeper, harder, and more principled than the easy satisfactions which are to be had from viewing glossy television advertisements in technicolour.

5

'Inclusive Development' and the Quintile Income Statistic*

Introduction

E very season has its buzzword, and the vogue today, it would appear, is 'inclusive development'. One supposes that the term is intended to cover a multitude of desirable aims and goals. As such, it seems reasonable to believe, for instance, that 'inclusive development' would have implications for the notions of 'national integration' and 'citizenship', and therefore for recent events on the ground in Jammu and Kashmir, the North-East, and the so-called 'Maoist Belt'. Similarly, one must expect that an engagement with 'inclusive development' must imply also an engagement with various manifestations of social exclusion based—for example—on caste, religious and gender identities. A third area of relevance would presumably relate to the extent—measured by both depth and coverage—of social security provisioning for the deprived. This is just a minute sample of the objects of concern of the term under discussion, but the sample is large enough to highlight certain elementary distinctions and contrasts.

* This essay appeared in *Economic and Political Weekly*, XLVI(4) (24 January 2011): 69–72.

In particular, it is impossible not to see that there is engagement in principle and disengagement in practice, just as there are pretty phrases and ugly facts. Thus, for many, the state's protestations of 'inclusive development' make for a clanging, jangling discord when juxtaposed with talk of sedition and anti-national activity; with the facts of manual scavenging, the socio-economic status of Muslims (as revealed in the Sachar Committee's report), and the scale of sex-selective foeticide in the country; and with the widespread perception that the unique identification programme which has been advertised as facilitating the 'targeting' of public benefits is, on the contrary, a mechanism for *excluding* large numbers of deserving citizens from the ambit of social assistance (when it is not associated with more sinister forms of intrusive surveillance of the citizenry). But we live in the age of the specialist, and it may not be for me to dwell at any length on these subjects. Having said this, it is also true that a further area of concern when we speak of 'inclusive development' relates to the domains of poverty, inequality and growth. This is a matter on which—for my sins as an economist—I might actually have something to say. (A good part of what I say here will draw heavily on Subramanian 2010.)

The Quintile Income

Summary statistics encapsulated in simple social indicators must not be expected to communicate complex and nuanced truths. Subject to this caveat, it is nevertheless useful to ask if one can think of an uncomplicated measure which, however imperfectly, might be expected to convey some information, all at once, on the phenomena of poverty, inequality and growth. My submission is that a useful index serving this purpose has, in earlier work, been advanced by Kaushik Basu (2001, 2006)—an index that he calls the '*quintile income*', or the average income of the poorest 20 per cent of a population. Basu proposes good reasons for why it would be appropriate to see the maximization of the quintile income as a legitimate goal of development. My intention in this note is to further advance the virtues of this simple measure (while being

mindful of its specific limitations, and also of the general limitations of the broader project of measurement). I would like to suggest that the Government should commit itself to a target rate of
growth of the quintile income, and that the *Economic Survey* should
provide statistics on a time-series of the quintile income (or rather
quintile consumption expenditure level, given that data on income
distribution are not systematically available for India). This form of
pre-commitment which is subject to public monitoring and collective scrutiny may just conceivably serve as an incentive for the
state to adopt some genuinely inclusive measures of governance.
Such measures—if one may dare to hope—should be concerned
not only with short-term policy initiatives but with longer-term
value orientations (entailing engagement with certain currently
seriously disfavoured instruments—such as land reform, increased
public spending, enhanced direct taxation and a tough line on
unaccounted money—for securing a more equitable social order).

Growth and Equity

Let me briefly explain how one may employ the quintile income as
a device for gauging and monitoring performance with respect to
poverty, inequality and growth. Consider the data on the growth
rate of per capita average consumption expenditure and average
consumption expenditure of the poorest 20 per cent of the population in India from 1977–78 to 2004–05. Some of the information
on trends in the mean consumption (call it M) and in the quintile
income (call it Q) for rural India are available in Tables 2 and 3
of Subramanian (2009), whose own computations are based on
the relevant National Sample Survey Organization's quinquennial
consumption expenditure surveys. Employing the Consumer Price
Index of agricultural labourers as a price deflator (for illustrative
purposes, and therefore not with a view to discouraging the quest
for deflators that might be more appropriate for the poorest 20 per
cent of the population), one obtains the summary statistics on the
mean per capita and quintile per capita consumption figures presented in Table 5.1.

Table 5.1

Average Per Capita and Quintile Consumption Expenditure Levels in Rural India: 1977–78 and 2004–05

Statistic	1977–78	2004–05
Mean per capita consumption in Rupees, at 1977–78 prices (M)	68.69	90.35
Quintile consumption in Rupees, at 1977–78 prices (Q)	29.14	44.91

Source: Calculations based on data in National Sample Survey Organization: *Report on the Second Quinquennial Survey on Consumer Expenditure*, Report No. 311, 32nd Round, July 1977–June 1978 and Household *Consumer Expenditure in India*, Report No. 505, 60th Round, January–June 2004.

It can be verified from the figures in Table 1 that the compound annual rate of growth in M over the 27-year period from 1977–78 to 2004–05 is 1.01 per cent, while the corresponding growth rate for Q is 1.62 per cent. It might appear that the definitely higher growth rate of Q compared to that of M is a symptom of considerably egalitarian or inclusive growth, but before we come to that conclusion, it is instructive also to take into account the *base* with respect to which growth rates are computed: consider the case of a two-person distribution (1,100) in period 1 which becomes (2,105) in period 2—five-sixth of the additional income generated goes to the richer person, though the growth rate of his income is only 5 per cent, while the growth rate of the poorer person's income is 100 per cent! In this context, it is useful to recall Serge Christophe Kolm's (1976a,b) distinction between 'rightist' and 'leftist' inequality measures: rightist measures are 'scale-invariant', that is, their value is unchanged if all incomes are scaled up or down by a given factor, while 'leftist' measures are 'translation-invariant', that is, their value remains the same if all incomes are increased or decreased by the same amount. Without in any way urging on the reader an unqualified acceptance of the supposed merits of translation invariance, it is nevertheless fair to point out that the appeal of scale-invariance has tended to be generally and uncritically accepted as being beyond question.

On Modestly 'Inclusive' Growth

In assessing what might constitute 'pro-poor' or 'inclusive' growth, it is useful to consider, by way of analogy, the problem of optimal budgetary intervention in poverty alleviation schemes. The problem in question is the one of identifying the poverty-minimizing pattern of allocation of a fixed budget among the poor, subject to the constraints that no poor person receives a sum in excess of her poverty gap and that no poor person is taxed. The solution to this problem would obviously depend upon the objective function—here subsumed in the poverty measure itself. Without getting into the details of the solutions to this programming problem, it is useful to note that the class of 'egalitarian' solutions could be seen to be constituted by those outcomes for which the poorer of two poor persons never gets a smaller share of the budget. The least egalitarian of the possible egalitarian outcomes then would be one in which each person receives an equal share of the budgetary provision available. (Contrast this with the more egalitarian outcome in which the poor receive transfers in proportion to their respective shortfalls from the poverty line. An even more equality-embracing outcome is the so-called 'Rawlsian' lexicographic maximin solution in which, starting with the poorest of the poor, we have a sequence of progressive and income-equalizing transfers until all the poor are raised to the maximum possible income that is compatible with the size of the budget, with the rest receiving no transfer at all.)

In a similar spirit, consider the problem of allocating, among the population of an economy, the 'budget' yielded by the growth of the economy's national income. Imagine that the economy has a population of n^1 and a mean income of M^1 in some initial period 1, which increase, respectively, to a population of n^2 and a mean income of M^2 in some subsequent period 2. (We employ 'income' interchangeably with 'consumption expenditure' here.) The aggregate levels of income in the two periods are then given, respectively, by $Y^1 = n^1 M^1$ and $Y^2 = n^2 M^2$, and the increase in aggregate income over the two time periods is the quantity $\Delta \equiv Y^2 - Y^1$. We can now imagine that we are in a situation similar to the one of optimal budgetary intervention for poverty alleviation. (It is as though the poverty line were several times larger than the richest person's income, so that we are effectively treating the entire population as potentially eligible for budgetary assistance.) In particular, we can ask: of all the possible 'egalitarian' distributions of Δ, which is the least egalitarian? (By an 'egalitarian distribution of Δ', we simply mean one in which the poorer of two income quantiles never gets a smaller share of the fruit of growth.) Suppose we decide, as a practical matter of convenience, to divide the population into quintiles, then the least egalitarian of the 'egalitarian' (or 'pro-poor' or 'inclusive') stratagems available for the distribution of Δ is one in which each quintile receives a share of $\Delta/5$ (a stratagem that could be seen to be a weakened version of what Stephan Klasen (2008) has called 'strong absolute pro-poor growth'). In particular, if q_1^1 and q_1^2 are the sizes of the quintile population in the base and terminal years, respectively, and Q_1^1 and Q_1^2 are the respective quintile incomes in the two years, then the aggregate incomes of the poorest quintile in the two years are given, respectively, by $Y_1^1 = q_1^1 Q_1^1$ and $Y_1^2 = q_1^2 Q_1^2$: the increase in the aggregate income of the poorest quintile is then $\Delta_1 \equiv Y_1^2 - Y_1^1$, and the modestly inclusive allocation strategy we suggest requires that $\Delta_1 = \Delta/5$.

The Indian Record: Some Elementary Illustrative Figures

Let us use the term 'warranted rate of growth' for the growth rate in the quintile income over two points in time which is compatible with implementation of the 'modestly inclusive growth' outcome just reviewed. The warranted rate of growth, that is, is the rate of growth in the quintile income that would obtain if the poorest quintile received a fifth share of the aggregate increase in income brought about by the growth process. We can compute the warranted rate of growth of the quintile consumption expenditure for India over the period from 1977–78 to 2004–05: this requires some very simple, but also boring, calculations to be performed, and these have accordingly been relegated to an appendix at the end of the note. The calculations in the appendix suggest that the 'warranted' compound annual rate of growth of the quintile consumption expenditure over the 27-year period from 1977–78 to 2004–05 is a modest 3.03 per cent, while the actual growth rate, at 1.62 per cent, is just a little over one-half the warranted growth rate. It is worth noting that what we call the warranted or desired growth rate corresponds to just the least egalitarian of the class of egalitarian distributions of the product of growth available. The achievement in this regard, therefore, turns out to be a modest fraction of a pedestrian goal.

Another Way of Reckoning the Problem

The arithmetic just discussed can be viewed in an alternative fashion. If g is the simple rate of growth of average *per caput* consumption expenditure over two years, and if g_1, g_2, g_3, g_4, and g_5 are the respective growth rates over these years of the average expenditure levels of the first, second, third, fourth and fifth poorest quintiles, while s_1^1, s_2^1, s_3^1, s_4^1, and s_5^1 are the respective expenditure shares of these quintiles in the base year, then it can be shown that the aggregate growth rate is a weighted sum of the quintile-specific growth rates, the weights being the quintile-specific expenditure shares: $g = s_1^1 g_1 + s_2^1 g_2 + s_3^1 g_3 + s_4^1 g_4 + s_5^1 g_5$. It follows from this, specifically, that the proportionate contribution of the poorest quintile to aggregate growth—call it c_1 —is given by $c_1 = s_1^1 g_1 / g$. In a 'neutral' growth regime, that is, one in which no quintile is favoured nor discriminated against, one would expect that $c_1 = c_2 = c_3 = c_4 = c_5 = 0.2$. Notice now that $c_1 = 0.2$ implies that $s_1^1 g_1 / g = 0.2$, or $g_1 = 0.2g / s_1^1$, or (noting that $s_1^1 = Y_1^1 / Y^1$) $g_1 = 0.2gY^1 / Y_1^1$, or $g_1 Y_1^1 = 0.2gY^1$ or (noting that $g_1 Y_1^1 \equiv \Delta_1$ and $gY^1 \equiv \Delta$), $\Delta_1 = \Delta / 5$ —which is precisely the allocation strategy dictated by the least egalitarian of the various egalitarian solutions that are available. As it happens, and if we treat 1977–78 and 2004–05 as the base year and the terminal year, respectively, the actual value of c_1 turns out to be just 0.145—less than three-quarters the value, 0.2, which it would have attained in a purely 'neutral' growth regime. This is an alternative way of asserting the earlier proposition that the actual achievement reflected by the Indian record is a modest fraction of a pedestrian goal.

There is no reason why the goal itself should be so pedestrian. While the Government's obsession with the growth in per capita national income is everywhere in evidence, one also encounters a conspicuous silence when it comes to proposing targeted rates of growth of the income of lower percentiles of the population. Indeed, it turns out that if we treat 2004–05 as the base year, employ the data available in Table 1 on the per capita consumption expenditure and quintile consumption expenditure levels in 2004–05, and project India's rural population in 2019–20 on the basis of the annual compound rate of growth of the country's rural population between 1991 and 2001, then a targeted compound annual rate of growth of, say, 5 per cent in average per capita consumption over the 15-year period from 2004–05 to 2019–20 would call forth a warranted compound annual rate of growth of the quintile consumption of the order of 8.4 per cent—when the actual historical record has been just 1.62 per cent per annum from 1977–78 to 2004–05, as reported earlier!

The Link with Poverty

The quintile income statistic can actually be rationalized, after a fashion, as a 'fuzzy' poverty measure, as has been sought to be done by Subramanian (2009 *op. cit.*). More directly, and inasmuch as the quintile income is concerned with the performance of the poorest 20 per cent of a population, there is a sense in which this statistic is transparently related to the notion of income poverty. Indeed, the measure is advanced by Subramanian (2009 *op. cit.*) as a practical and simple alternative to poverty measures derived through the more conventional 'identification-cum-aggregation' route. This is in no way to deny that the quintile income, viewed as a measure of poverty, is marked by several conceptual problems. But then, conceptual difficulties also preside over each of the identification and aggregation exercises of the conventional approach to poverty measurement. Indeed, the problems involved are so severe that when it comes to assessing trends in money-metric poverty in India, equally plausible variations on a theme of identification yield, over the period from 1977–78 to 2004–05, both (a) a substantially declining trend in poverty (as reflected in official estimates), and (b) an increasing trend (as reflected in the estimates of Utsa Patnaik 2007). The truth is probably in between, as reflected in the performance of the quintile income, which suggests a slow and laboured over-time improvement on a very low base. Even if official poverty estimates are not to be supplanted by estimates of the quintile income, one could at least ask for the one set of estimates to be supplemented by the other. The trend in the quintile income should itself serve to cast doubt on claims of dramatic improvements on the poverty front. In the end, the case for the quintile income does not have to be predicated on the (plainly unsustainable) judgement that it is the most appealing index of poverty available: a sufficient advertisement in its cause should be the proposition that it is a plausible and useful indicator of poverty.

Conclusion

In this note I have listed a small sample of areas in which the notion of inclusive development would find ready application. The intention has been to urge that the appropriate response to these troublesome aspects of inclusive development resides in some minimally serious engagement with the problem, rather than in the debater's points that can be so easily scored by securing the services of clever spin doctors. In a general way, from the perspectives of both political morality and enlightened self-interest, there is a case against obtruding a wedge between popular slogans and actual reality. It would be a pity if 'inclusive development' were to go the way of other distinguished predecessors of the catchy phrase. One of them, it may be recalled, is 'India Shining'.

In a more specific context, there may be something to be said for measuring money-metric poverty in terms of the quintile income statistic and of monitoring its performance by setting targeted rates of growth for the statistic, in accordance with clearly articulated patterns of pro-poor growth and of at least modestly equitable distribution of the anticipated product of growth. The claim is not that such a view of poverty is exempt from conceptual niggles. But then neither is the more conventional approach of identification and aggregation so exempt. Apart from this, the alternative proposal is amenable to simple and straightforward interpretation; it incorporates a workable notion of 'inclusive growth'; and it is not easily vulnerable to the temptations of manipulation.

Appendix

Some Simple Calculations to Derive the 'Warranted' Rate of Growth of the Quintile Income

In the light of the considerations informing the proposal for a 'modestly inclusive'. distribution of the product of growth, employing the superscripts 1 and 2 for the years 1977–78 and 2004–05, respectively, using information on the size of India's rural population from the *Provisional Population Tables of the Census of India 2001*, expressing all monetary values at 1977–78 prices, and making use of the figures available in Table 5.1, we note that $n^1 = 496.87$ millions; $n^2 = 786.5$ millions; $M^1 = ₹68.89$; $M^2 = ₹90.35$; $Y^1 (= n^1M^1) = ₹34,229$ millions; $Y^2 (= n^2M^2) = ₹71,060$ millions and $\Delta (\equiv Y^2 - Y^1) = ₹36,831$ millions. The share of Δ which, according to the least egalitarian of the available egalitarian distributions, should go to the poorest quintile is $\Delta/5$, which works out to ₹7,366 millions. The total income of the poorest quintile in 2004–05 ought then to be the sum of its equal share of the fruit of growth (₹7,366 millions) and its total income in 1977–78 (which is the product of the 1977–78 quintile income of ₹29.14 and the 1977–78 quintile population of 99.37 millions, which is ₹2,896 millions). The total 'desired' aggregate income of the poorest quintile in 2004–05 is then

₹7,366 millions + ₹2,896 millions = ₹10,262 millions, whence the 'desired' quintile income in 2004–05 is the desired total income of the poorest quintile in 2004–05 divided by the 2004–05 quintile population of 157.3 millions, or ₹65.24. To summarize: the actual quintile incomes in 1977–78 and 2004–05, at 1977–78 prices, were ₹29.14 and ₹44.91. The 'desired' or 'warranted' quintile income in 2004–05, at 1977–78 prices, is ₹65.24. An increase in the quintile income from ₹29.14 in 1977–78 to ₹65.24 in 2004–05 implies a 'warranted' annual compound rate of growth in the quintile income of 3.03 per cent.

References

Basu, K. (2001), 'On the Goals of Development', in G.M. Meier and J.E. Stiglitz (eds), *Frontiers of Development Economics: The Future in Perspective*. New York: Oxford University Press.

———. (2006), 'Globalization, Poverty, and Inequality: What is the Relationship? What Can be Done?', *World Development*, 34(8): 1361–73.

Klasen, S. (2008), 'Economic Growth and Poverty Reduction: Measurement Issues Using Income and Non-Income Indicators', *World Development*, 36(3): 420–45.

Kolm, S.C. (1976a), 'Unequal Inequalities: I', *Journal of Economic Theory*, 12(3): 416–42.

———. (1976b), 'Unequal Inequalities: II', *Journal of Economic Theory*, 13(1): 82–111.

Patnaik, U. (2007), 'Neoliberalism and Rural Poverty in India', *Economic and Political Weekly*, 48(32): 3132–50.

Subramanian, S. (2009), 'A Practical Proposal for Simplifying the Measurement of Income Poverty', in K. Basu and R. Kanbur (eds), *Arguments for a Better World: Essays in Honour of Amartya Sen, Volume 1: Ethics, Welfare, and Measurement*. Clarendon: Oxford University Press.

Subramanian, S. (2010), 'Identifying the Income-Poor: Some Controversies in India and Elsewhere', Courant Research Centre 'Poverty, Equity and Growth', Discussion Paper No. 46, November, Goettingen.

Polity and Society

6
Reprisal without Rectitude*

The dreadful violence visited upon thousands of innocent civilians in the cities of New York and Washington, DC, on the 11th of September, has shaken the world, and moved its citizens to horror over the events, condemnation of the perpetrators, and sympathy with the victims. The feeling has been genuine, spontaneous and overwhelming. This tragic circumstance, in the immediate aftermath of its occurrence, brought the world together, in a commonly shared revulsion against the tactics of terrorism, and a concerted resolve to counter it globally. It was a rare moment of reaching out and coming together, of discovering a shared sense of humane fellow feeling and consolidated purpose.

The United States, and some of its more strident allies (notably the United Kingdom), would have done well to seize the moment. It would have been the beginning of wisdom, and compatible with a gracious acceptance of the widespread expression of support and solidarity that has been in evidence, for the US to carry the rest of the world with it, in a spirit of mutuality, consultation and deferral. What, instead, has been on display over the last week is a certain familiar exhibition of subjectivism, hubris and unilateral statement of intent. Consider, in this context, the on-going preparations for

---

*This essay was written in September 2001 and rejected by a national newspaper—on the grounds, as I came to understand, that my proper place was to confine myself to commentaries on the annual Budget and similar phenomena.

a military strike against Afghanistan, which without a doubt will entail the most horrendous hardship for hundreds of thousands of innocent Afghan civilians (many of whom are already fleeing to the closed borders with Pakistan); the extraordinary moral argument which holds the Sadam Hussains and the Talibans accountable for the devastation that might be unleashed on Iraqi or Afghan citizens by the West's military offensives against their countries; the demonization of allegedly Islamic fundamentalism through the well-worn stratagem of equipping it with an identifiable name and face (subsumed, in this instance, in the persona of Osama bin Laden) in a general climate of uncertainty, speculation and partial knowledge regarding agency; the repeated assertions of moral superiority of the 'civilized world' vis-à-vis the presumably underdeveloped ethical sensibility of much of the Third World; the media's ceaseless emphasis on contrasting 'our' values with 'theirs', as manifest, for example, in the BBC's hectoring, badgering tone (a prominent PLO leader's condemnation of the terrorist attack on America is met with the suggestion that this might be a case of too little too late; protesting Pakistani citizens are referred to as 'noisy pockets' that have decided to cast their lot with 'the Islamic Taliban against the Christian West'). None of these responses, regrettably, strikes an authentic note of righteousness, and none does the least justice to those that have tragically lost their lives and those that are now and henceforth expected to lose theirs in payment.

Anger and grief can, and must, be understood. The passion of the wronged and injured asks to be met with compassionate comprehension. But there is an incalculable strain placed on the prospects of such reasoned acceptance when the legitimacy of passion and anger is always, and only, asserted on the one side of the ledger, and never on the other. In a slightly more even-handed treatment of claims and interests than America and England have succeeded in projecting, there must be room for an acceptance and acknowledgement of facts such as the following ones. The US has to its credit the fact of securing a very high standard of living for the bulk of its citizens: one applauds this country's achievement in this regard. But if passion is to be permitted its say, it must also be recorded that this is a country whose indigenous native population was virtually decimated (and whose survivors are now confined to reservations), with a savagery that has been captured as well as might reasonably be expected, through the artistic enterprise of an institution called Hollywood, for the edification of its citizens. This country exploded a nuclear device (for the first and last time on an actual living population in the history of the world) over two Japanese cities. It carpet-bombed Viet Nam and sent thousands of civilians screaming to their deaths through an instrument called napalm. Its officers and gentlemen participated in a massacre which has become part of the history and geography of the world called My Lai. It must be further recorded that any little breast-beating these brutalities may have provoked was shown up for being the cissiness it represented, in the form of further celebratory justifications that were offered up by Hollywood, in the persona of a certain Rambo, for the harmless entertainment of patriots looking out for some innocent pleasure. One of the multinational corporations of this country, in a minor aside to the pursuit of profit, got mixed up in a bit of a nuisance concerning the death and crippling of a few thousand people through poison gas leaking out of its factory in a city called Bhopal. This country, it may also be recalled, led a force that appointed itself to save humanity from a monster called Saddam Hussein, in which cause more than hundred thousand Iraqis were killed in missile attacks and a million children were starved through economic blockades.

If the United Nations Organization has been a conspicuously feeble actor in the many infractions of global peace we are being continually exposed to, it is hard to lay the blame only and entirely on a Third World brutality which has cynically outflanked the lofty moralism of the UN, as reflected in various acts of vicious internal war in locales such as Kosovo, Liberia, Sierra Leone or Somalia. Other passions, and other demands for truth and justice, must be expected to raise questions regarding super-power-sponsored assassination attempts on Fidel Castro and Muammar Gaddafi; the Iran-contra war in Nicaragua; the invasion of Granada's sovereignty; and the attacks on Iraq, Kosovo, Sudan and Palestine.

There has been much talk of 'evil' in the aftermath of the terrorist attacks on America. No, the idea is not to exonerate evil here by reference to evil there. But it is to draw reference to the tasteless insensitivity of what, at its most benign, is a continuing form of the theme of White Man's Burden emanating from the US, the UK and some of their allies. An enquiry into evil is mediated by a more secular and a more inclusively humanistic temper than is afforded by some crude mixture of petulance, superiority, one-sidedness and a morality that refuses to make any concession whatever to the universalisability of principles of right conduct.

I would, in the light of the foregoing, urge the governments and the peoples of the 'Western alliance' to proceed with greater restraint, tolerance and patience than has hitherto been in evidence. I would also urge the Government of India to desist, at all costs, from offering military or logistical support to unilateral declarations of war, outside the framework of UN resolutions, by one bloc of countries on another. What extraordinary delusion of grandeur, it may be asked, prompts me to offer advice and consent to the mighty nations of this world? None whatever. I freely concede that I am an anonymous nobody in the scheme of things; and there is, in the concession, no desire to make a virtue of necessity. But there is a certain moral force vouchsafed to my view, and to that of millions of my fellow nobodies, that emanates from the privileges and responsibilities which are associated with the fact that we happen to be citizens of our respective countries, and citizens of this world. That moral force, of course, is quite easily denied, and even trampled upon—an act which would stand testimony not to righteousness but merely to power.

7

Moral Catastrophes and Immoral Reasoning*

In the aftermath of the dreadful carnage in Gujarat, and in the course of the continuing violence witnessed in that state, many people have spoken out against these terrible happenings in loud, clear voices of pain, anger, and denunciation. Ordinary citizens, activists, political parties, the media, scholars, and professionals—all of these agencies have joined their voices against the forces that seek legitimacy for state-abetted communal pogroms, ethnic cleansing, and genocide. Every one of these voices that has spoken, when we have not, deserves our humble acknowledgement and gratitude. For it is thanks to these voices that we now have at least an audible murmur in place of the deafening silence that might so easily have come to pass if there had been universal subscription to the sort of moral reasoning that seems to mediate the refined quietness of such large sections of the literate upper middle class-and-above population of this country.

It is of this silence from this quarter that I wish to speak: the silence that informs ordinary conversation among friends and acquaintances; the silence of large chunks of the regional written media; the silence of influential men and women in public affairs; the silence of academic institutions which one might have expected to serve

* This essay appeared in *Economic and Political Weekly*, 37(26): 2567–9, 29 June–2 July 2002.

as 'natural' sources of principled and intellectual opposition to wrongdoing. It would be helpful if this essay could be seen as being directed at, rather than against, these sources of silence, not least because this essay is in some measure an exercise in talking to oneself, in addressing a problem of which the author is himself a part rather than outside of it. Despite this *caveat*, it will not be surprising if what is on offer ends up attracting those strictures that are specially reserved for the sins of didacticism and preachiness. But the matter at hand is too important for one to shrink from the prospect of being called moralistic: it is a small price to pay in the face of the mor(t)al horrors that confront us today. Apart from which, there might, after all, be something to be said for suspending judgement on who is, and who is not, really guilty of self-righteousness: there is just the possibility that those who see their silence as a principled refusal to be holier-than-thou are persistently judging you for judging without the humility that so thoroughly informs their own modest and civilized abstention from noisiness.

*

In conversations with friends, neighbours and acquaintances, one perceives a certain self-conscious effort at avoiding the topic of Gujarat. Not that there is any particular virtue, seen in the light of sufficient intervention, in talking of the subject. It is just that—as a matter of necessary involvement—unless there is some persistent engagement with the subject, in thought and in speech, it is hard to see one's way to any sort of meaningful intervention in the matter. If the topic should still be determinedly insinuated into the conversation, a commonly encountered piece of reasoning for not pursuing it further assumes the following form: 'What's the good of talking about it? Where's the point? One's views are not going to make the least difference to what's happening (Pause.) Are you going to stick around during the vacation?'

There are two grand traditions in moral reasoning: the *consequentialist* tradition and the *deontic* tradition. In terms of the first system, actions are judged according to their consequences. In terms

of the second, actions are judged not according to their consequences but according to prior moral principles of obligation and
onus. *Utilitarianism* is an example of a consequentialist philosophy:
that action is to be commended, according to this philosophy,
which brings about the consequence of a higher sum total of utility for the members of a society. Moses' Ten Commandments, and
Kant's 'categorical moral imperatives', are examples of deontic systems of moral thought: the commandments and imperatives place
constraints on one's actions not from any consequentialist line of
reasoning, but from foundational considerations of right conduct.
Whether or not we are self-consciously aware of it, much of our
own moral reasoning is guided by some combination of consequentialist and deontic considerations.

It is a matter of some importance to be clear about which line of
reasoning we choose to invoke under what circumstances. When
someone says 'What's the good of talking about Gujarat?', she/he
is invoking a consequentialist argument. This strikes me as being
thoroughly misplaced. One does not talk about Gujarat because
it may (or may not) do any 'good:' one engages with the subject
because it is right to do so, or at any rate, because it would be
wrong to avoid it wholesale.

It's no thanks to people who ask 'What's the good of voting?'
that this country, despite all its monstrous iniquities and imperfec-
tions, is still something of a functioning democracy. The disabled
old lady who has to be carried on her son's back over a distance
of 20 kilometres under a scorching sun to the polling booth casts
her vote because it is her right and her duty to do so, not because
she believes in the silly superstition (which it would be natural
to associate with her benighted status of illiterate ignorance) that
her one solitary vote from among a few hundred million votes is
going to make any blessed difference at the margin. Her example
is a humbling one, and should appeal in particular to the humility
of those who, apart from the consequentialist futility of speaking
up, are also seized, as a justification for their silence, by the deontic
principle that commands: 'Thou shalt not judge.' Not judge when
what's at stake is state-supported killing and lynching of targeted
communities? Even a die-hard supporter of deontological ethics

like the American philosopher Robert Nozick has conceded that deontic reasoning must yield place to consequentialist reasoning in the face of what he calls 'moral catastrophes'. By employing consequentialist categories when deontic ones are more apposite to the issue at hand, and, contrariwise, deontic principles when consequentialist ones are in order, there is a fine confusion of the logic of morality on display in arriving at the decision that silence is an acceptable option to implement.

Additionally, and in the interests of consistency, if it is in order to ask 'What's the good of talking about Gujarat?', it should also be in order to ask 'What's the good of not doing so?' As far as I can tell, the 'good' would reside in the saving of a little bit of private bother, some personal inconvenience. There is a certain dull lack of nobility in this 'good' which one must be forgiven for finding less than wholly inspiring.

*

A second line of argumentation is that of the 'realist school' which invites you to see the facts of life, a *machismo* acceptance of which will convince you of the embarrassingly pathetic exhibition of blubbery idealism you are guilty of when you breathe recrimination and demand rectification. Specifically, it is out of court, in this view, to condemn the DMK and the Trinamool Congress for voting with the Government in the Lok Sabha, to criticize the AIADMK for abstaining and to find fault with the TDP for staging an opportunistic walkout after days of 'will-they, won't-they?' teasing. There are two strands to this line of reasoning: first, it could be ill-judged to castigate political parties without a sufficient appreciation of their political compulsions; and second, what about the rest of the opposition?—it is not as if they are acting the way they are for reasons of purity of heart, rather than in order to make political capital out of what has happened in Gujarat.

I will try and take the two strands in order. I do not believe there is anything particularly hard-nosed, street-savvy, or man-of-the-world-ish in understanding the political compulsions of political parties. The calculus of cynicism is transparent enough and simple enough for a child to grasp. No elaborate lectures are really required to explain why political parties have acted the way they have. But in moral reasoning I believe there is a strong case for differentiating between reason as causation and reason as justification. If a political party with a strong tradition of rationalism and social justice decides to go with the Government on the Gujarat issue, it requires no great cerebral feat to infer that considerations of political survival have inspired the decision. One can see reason as causation readily enough. One cannot even begin to see reason as justification, though. It does not make it right, or acceptable, or deserving of sympathetic understanding that the political party acted as it did because its own strategies of survival dictated that it should so act. The gradual and oftentimes unconscious assimilation of reason as causation into the category of reason as justification has a dangerous proclivity for blurring the distinction between fact and evaluation. This just will not do. I recall an incident involving my late friend S. Guhan, who could be accused of many things, but not the vice of being impractical or wanting in a pragmatic appreciation of the world and its ways. After receiving a host of predictable and commonplace criticisms regarding the political feasibility of a social security package he had proposed at a seminar, he responded thus: 'Someone has to do something for the silent poor. We are not talking of what the politicians are likely to do. It is obviously because they are not likely to do it that I thought it was the responsibility of academics to press for it.' Such a position stems not from a failure to comprehend politics, but from the success of comprehending it only too well. Sometimes, to understand all is to forgive nothing.

The second strand of the argument. Because I condemn the DMK, etc., does not mean I am a Congress-wallah or a CPM supporter. There are plenty of sticks to beat these political parties with, and no doubt they should be wielded at the appropriate time and in the appropriate context. But I should see it as being worse than diversionary to question these parties' purity of heart and nobility of intent at *this* juncture; however, little faith I may have in either. Such an undifferentiated assault is misguided in the present context, it loses the pointed edge of relevance and it ultimately muddies the prospect of uniting forces against an evil that both cries out to be swiftly stopped in its tracks and cannot possibly be tolerated. The plain fact of the matter (and it is a wonder that it has been missed by the realists!) is that the battle lines were drawn in Parliament following on a clear division of positions with respect to a matter of profound importance for the security of a subset of this country's citizens: it just so happens that a large segment of the opposition—whatever its intrinsic character—was on the side of the angels. Under *these proximate circumstances*, where one is faced by a referendum-like situation, I should be inclined to assert my disapprobation for those who went along with the Government, without being starry-eyed about those went against it. One may be no votary of the Congress Party, but this fact need not in any way diminish one's disgust at the Defense Minister's view that, contrary to the stories that were being bruited, Gujarat was not the first instance of pregnant women having their foetuses plucked out of their wombs to be thrown into the fire.

Finally, in respect of both strands of the 'realist school's' argument, it is instructive not to forget what the stakes are. These, to repeat, are state-supported genocide and ethnic cleansing. In brief: a moral catastrophe.

*

A third line of reasoning has to do with the perceived wisdom of not taking issues like Gujarat too 'personally:' it is the sort of thing that can jeopardize objectivity, compromise stability and lead to harsh and hasty judgement. A cautious silence, in this view, is dictated by preserving a distance that lends perspective. *Is* there substance in the view that some people have taken the matter too 'personally'? Yes and No. Yes, in the sense that moral reasoning cannot be bereft of a sense of 'selfhood:' this theme constitutes an important part of Robert Bolt's play of Sir Thomas More, and I can do worse than quote him from his preface to *A Man For All Seasons*: '... [T]hough few of us have anything in ourselves like an immortal soul which we regard as absolutely inviolable, yet most of us still feel something which we should prefer, on the whole, not to violate. ... I think the paramount gift our thinkers, artists, and for all I know, our men of science, should labour to get for us is a sense of selfhood ... .' Yes, it is intimately personal in this sense. And yet, also wholly impersonal, because the notion of self-hood is being urged on every sentient agent as a universal, practical prescription for right conduct. Our selves cannot but be welded together, in a union of the personal and the universal, when we stare a moral catastrophe like Gujarat in the face.

*

A fourth sort of justification for silence resides in placing a great distance between the perpetrators of the Gujarat crimes and one-self: the former do not represent the latter, and there can be no question of taking responsibility for the inconceivably monstrous acts of people that one has never had any truck with. It seems to me that there are two sorts of response that are in order here. The first has to do with the notion that whatever the (real or imagined) distance between the perpetrators of the Gujarat outrage and one-self, there can be no such distance between the *victims* of that out-rage and oneself. The Muslim minorities that have been stabbed and torched and driven out of their homes are our brothers and sisters: they are ours to defend and to protect; and considerations of solidarity with them in their horrifying predicament require us to speak up, for reasons of the rightness of assuming responsibility, even if not necessarily guilt. A second response is that fighting the forces of evil is not most effectively done by perceiving an incal-culable distance between those forces and ourselves: they are not as far from us as we may comfortably assume, and the danger of silence is the danger of being eventually assimilated into that evil. There is reason to forfeit the complacence of a silence fathered by the imagined distance between oneself and a moral catastrophe around one: the reason is the message of William Golding's *Lord of the Flies*, in which the boy Simon dies trying to save his friends with the discovery of the truth that 'the Beast is in us'.

*

A fifth, and rather more sinister, reason for silence is a gradual accession to the relentlessly insidious thesis that has infiltrated the public consciousness, the thesis that suggests that radical thought and a secular outlook have systematically eroded the legitimate rights of the majority community and paved the way for a natural (even if slightly regrettable) reprisal such as has been witnessed in Gujarat. A typical example of this repugnant variety of 'reasoning' offers the view that the persistent attempt at seeing society as being dominated by 'upper classes' and 'upper castes' has driven good and moderate Hindu leaders of an earlier vintage out of the political reckoning, to be replaced by phenomena like Narendra Modi; such divisiveness on the part of radicals and secularists has driven otherwise nationalistic members of the 'upper classes and castes' to seek employment with multinational companies or abroad; and more along the same lines—the idea being that Gujarat and allied happenings are an inevitable culmination of the excesses of a certain kind of politics that has stretched the tolerance of the majority community beyond endurance. The message is quite clear: if you will not brook the iniquities of the caste, class and communal divisions of this country, just wait and see how much worse it can and will get. The wages of resisting moral injustice are moral catastrophes—which you, and you alone, will have brought down upon your heads. This is substantially the position that was recently chillingly underlined by the RSS, and echoed (despite the subsequent 'clarifications', for which he has now become famous) in his warning to *jehadi* Muslims issued in Goa by the Prime Minister of this country. I confess myself unable to respond to this form of 'argumentation'; the problem I confront is a very elementary one, namely, that in this line of 'moral reasoning', there is neither morality nor reason to contend with.

*

There is a sixth reason for silence: quiet celebration, among certain quarters, of the Gujarat bloodbath. This is the most horrifying moral catastrophe of all.

8

Looking Back and Ahead*

A theory doing the rounds, in the immediate aftermath of the (2004) electoral verdict, is that India has voted against 'good economics and bad politics'. In these days of instant messaging and media bombardment, there is some danger of the theory attaining to the status of an eternal verity. It may be a losing battle to entertain the ambition that one can halt the transformation of catchy slogans into higher truths, but there is, after all, no harm in trying. In the cause of such an effort, the reader is invited to judge if she is easily able to decide which has been the more vulgar of two spectacles she has been exposed to on television in recent days. One is the spectacle of the politics of shaven heads, white saris and upper-caste widowhood. The other is the spectacle of the economics of baying stockbrokers and a tumbling stock market, enacted to the accompaniment of a hysterical, ball-by-ball description by media commentators. Both have been commonly united in a display of unrestrained antipathy towards Sonia Gandhi and

*This piece was written in May 2004, in the immediate aftermath of the General (Lok Sabha) Elections. The shelf life of an essay such as this is very short: a national daily to which the article was sent failed (or chose not) to respond, and in a matter of a week, it was not any longer topical enough to submit to any other newspaper. Parts of the essay were subsequently employed in the author's entry on 'Poverty' in Kaushik Basu (ed.) (2007), *Oxford Companion to Economics in India*. New Delhi: Oxford University Press; and parts were employed in a review of a book edited by Kaushik Basu (2004), *India's Emerging Economy: Performance and Prospects in the 1990s and Beyond*. Cambridge, MA: the MIT Press. The review appeared in *International Review of Economics and Finance*, 14(4): 495–7, 2005.

the new dispensation. And both, together, constitute an unmistakable postscript to five years of misrule, of bad politics and of bad economics. One cannot, of course, explain the electoral verdict without reference to the precise concatenation of electoral alliances and state-specific performances that have happened. Even so, the net outcome of the democratic process is one in which a regime which has presided over a combination of bad economics and bad politics has been voted out of power. On this score, we as a nation do deserve to congratulate ourselves.

That said, one still needs to address the following question: has the electorate really delivered a clear-cut, consciously thought-through verdict on the ideology of 'reform economics' on the one hand, and against the ideology of intolerantly fascist religious nationalism on the other? The answer is: probably not. A more realistic assessment, perhaps, is that there is a large enough constituency within the country which has been subjected to the felt experience of mass income-poverty, endemic hunger, starvation deaths, ill health, unemployment, and lack of access to water and energy. This constituency has refused to be diverted from its material predicament by 'cultural' appeals to divisive religious sentiment through the deployment of such instruments as targeted minority-bashing, the destruction of places of religious worship, anti-conversion laws, and state-abetted genocide. This is heartening enough, when set against the pre-election image of a swaggeringly assertive and supremely self-confident ruling alliance which had thought fit to advance the parliamentary elections in a spirit of getting a ritual with a preordained result out of the way before embarking on another five years of a more aggressive implementation of its ambitions. Heartening enough, but not a cause for either romanticism or complacence.

The new formation at the centre must therefore strain every nerve to ensure it does not repeat the mistakes of its predecessor or of those of its own major constituent in earlier times. The case for vigilance is not being advanced on the basis of some crudely 'strategic' or 'instrumental' reasoning revolving around the calculation of a one-to-one correspondence between policies/programmes and votes. In any event, the limits to canny strategizing would be quickly exposed by the uncertain and unpredictable influences of 'local conditions', charismatic leadership, and meteorological phenomena. Everything considered, there is a purely intrinsic case for good governance and enlightened administration. In this spirit, and largely by way of a laundry list of issues requiring urgent attention, but in no particular order of imputed importance, the following menu is offered for consideration.

First, both Godhra and its aftermath need to be swiftly put through an impartial judicial process: the need for 'closure', as the psychologists call it, invites immediate consideration. Second, if this is a time for reconstruction, it is also a time for systematic dismantling. The elaborate apparatus of communal politics, and its infiltration into every aspect of the educational system, needs to be quickly taken apart. From school textbooks to university curricula to the agenda and composition of institutions of higher learning, what is called for is a quick and efficient broom. The state to which the Indian Council of Historical Research, the Indian Council of Social Science Research, the Archaeological Survey of India, the University Grants Commission and the National Council of Educational Research and Training have degenerated would be laughable if it were not also so tragic. To guard against creating an impression of 'tit-for-tat' politics, of 'then-it-was-your turn, now-it-is-mine' tactics, it would be essential to create a complete archival record of the manner and methods by which the educational system has been sought to be subverted by the communal agendum, and to share this record with the public.

Third, poverty cannot be banished by simply banishing that word from one's political vocabulary. A strong pro-poor and anti-corruption signal can be sent out by recovering—at least in a few 'obvious' and egregious cases—unpaid taxes on income and wealth, and earmarking the proceeds specifically for poverty-alleviation purposes; and likewise by imposing a 'poverty surcharge' on personal and corporate income, with this component of direct taxation again set aside for anti-poverty measures. Fourth, the perversion of bursting public granaries coexisting with the phenomenon of chronic undernutrition intensifying, from time to time, into conditions of starvation, must be eliminated. The public distribution system must be restored, and improved. Fifth, poverty is often not just a matter of income deprivation: if one is interested in a serious assault on deprivation in its more generalized forms, it would help to draw a district-wise map of India, with the colour red reserved for those districts displaying acute inadequacies in the access to drinking water, energy for cooking, elementary health facilities, a school, and a road; and, on the basis of such a map, some prioritized effort at infrastructural development must be initiated and sought to be implemented under a reasonable time frame.

Sixth, the plethora of anti-poverty employment schemes must be rationalized and streamlined. Indeed, the principal merit of employment schemes resides in their 'self-selection' property, which obviates the necessity for costly targeting, but often employment schemes incur large administrative, overhead, and material costs; are subject to the machinations of corrupt contractors; and do not result in the creation of durable assets. There may therefore be a strong case for preserving the 'self-selection' property of wage employment schemes while reformulating some of them as adult literacy programmes (with an explicit value orientation, both for its own sake and as a corrective to the recent attempts at ill-conceived indoctrination), which can result in the creation of a durable social and human asset, and at the same time have a beneficent effect on fertility and child labour. Seventh, the 1991–96 Congress-led government was already in possession of a complete blueprint of a National Assistance Scheme, in devising which the late S. Guhan had played a major role: this is a feasible and affordable package of social security measures covering old age pension, survivor benefit, accident compensation and disability relief, which can be dusted, aired, implemented, and given the widest possible publicity, both to inform potential beneficiaries of their entitlements and to advertise serious intent.

An unrealistic wish list? Possibly, though one is inclined to believe not. This is the season of hope, the time for fresh beginnings. It cannot hurt to dream restrained dreams.

9
Examining the 'Creamy Layer' Principle*

COMMENTARY

Introduction

In a recent verdict, a Constitution Bench of the Supreme Court has upheld the validity of the 77th, 81st, 82nd and 85th Constitutional Amendments on reservation for Scheduled Castes (SCs) and Scheduled Tribes (STs) in the matter of promotion in government employment. This verdict has generated afresh a debate on the merits of the so-called 'creamy layer' criterion in determining eligibility to the benefits of affirmative action. Abstracting from the specificities of the judgement, a matter of general concern it provokes relates to the principle that in any scheme of group-based reservation, the 'creamy layer' ought to be excluded from preferential treatment. Indeed, this principle—which, for convenience, will here be called the 'creamy layer principle'—has been held

---

* Part I of this essay ('Examining the Creamy Layer Principle') was published in *Economic and Political Weekly*, 41(45): 4643–4, October 2006; and Part II ('A Reply to Sundaram and Ravi Srinivas') was published in *Economic and Political Weekly*, 42(4): 329–31, 27 January–2 February 2007). Both parts have been subsequently reprinted in: S. Thorat and N. Kumar (eds.): *In Search of Inclusive Policy: Assessing Graded Inequality*, Indian Institute of Dalit Studies and Rawat Publishers: New Delhi, 2008.

out by many forward caste persons as an argument against providing reservation in education to the 'creamy layer' segments of the 'backward castes'. Once the validity of the 'creamy layer principle' is acknowledged in any one dimension of application, or as an axiomatically appealing principle of equality at an abstract level, it would be inconsistent to deny its validity in other spheres of application. It therefore becomes a matter of some importance to submit the appeal of this principle to critical scrutiny.

One means to this end is to work through a particularly simple illustrative example and to examine the analytical implications it has for considerations of group equality. This is a method which Amartya Sen has called the 'case-implication method': it involves constructing counterfactual, though conceivable, situations and testing our moral intuition against the outcomes dictated by this or that principle when applied to this or that situation. The idea is not to build a complex and nuanced moral or political theory on the basis of a simple example, but rather, at a preliminary level, to provide an anchor for certain ideas which, at the present moment, are not exactly distinguished for their clarity or freedom from ambiguity.

One Judgement, One Assumption

With this in mind, let us imagine that society can be partitioned, along caste lines, into a backward caste (which has been historically discriminated against and oppressed) and a forward caste; and, along economic lines, into the poor and the rich. We are interested in assessing what sort of mechanism of compensatory discrimination might assist the cause of justice in the allocation of scarce educational opportunities among competing contenders for them. That is, whom, and to what extent, is a system of preferential treatment towards those who are disadvantaged by caste and/or income-deficiency likely to assist? To answer this question requires one to make some plausible judgements and assumptions. I shall make one judgement and one assumption. I shall judge that caste backwardness is a more crippling disability than is income insufficiency, and, in particular, that the 'capability gap' between a rich backward caste person and a rich forward caste person is greater than that between a poor forward caste person and an economically better-placed person of his own caste. Further, I shall assume that poor cohorts of the backward caste group would, because of their social and educational disadvantage, typically not fare academically well enough to be greatly aided by the availability of compensating concessions in their behalf. Under these circumstances, the implementation of a 'creamy layer corrective' is likely to exacerbate prevailing caste disparities in the access to education. The example furnished below is intended to illustrate this conclusion. It is important to stress that the example is just that—an example, whose role is to clarify a certain line of reasoning and not serve as a precise and literal replication of reality.

An Illustrative Example

Suppose, then, that four candidates appear for a competitive examination for admission to a professional college and that only two seats are available. Imagine that one of the candidates is a poor backward caste person (whom we shall refer to as PBC), one is a rich backward caste person (whom we shall refer to as RBC), one is a poor forward caste person (whom we shall refer to as PFC) and the fourth is a rich forward caste person (whom we shall refer to as RFC). Let it be the case that a candidate has to secure a mark of 80 per cent in order to qualify for admission. This, however, is only a necessary condition. Among those that qualify, only the two top-ranked candidates will be selected. In what follows, we consider a certain hypothetical distribution of marks among the four candidates, and alternative schemes of compensatory discrimination, together with the outcomes they lead to, in terms of the candidates selected.

Suppose the distribution of marks is as follows: 70 for PBC, 81 for RBC, 83 for PFC, and 85 for RFC. This distribution simulates the commonly observed phenomenon that, other things equal, academic performance improves with each of economic and caste status. Suppose, further, that *no* mechanism of compensatory discrimination is in place (Case I). Then, clearly, the selected candidates will be PFC and RFC. Next, suppose that we have a scheme of extra marks allotted to a person suffering from the disadvantage of caste backwardness (Case II); specifically, assume that a backward caste person is given six extra marks. Then, the 'effective' marks of PBC and RBC, respectively, will be 76 (= 70 + 6) and 87 (= 81 + 6), while the 'effective' marks of PFC and RFC will remain at 83 and 85, respectively. The chosen candidates, in this situation, will be RBC and RFC. Consider a third case (Case III), in which caste-based preferential treatment is given to a backward caste person (six extra marks), *but only if she/he happens to be poor:* this scheme upholds the 'creamy layer principle'. Then, the 'effective' marks of PBC, RBC, PFC and RFC will be, respectively, 76 (= 70 + 6), 81 (no extra marks for RBC because he belongs to the 'creamy layer' by virtue of being rich and is excluded from preferential treatment), 83, and 85. In this situation, the selected candidates will be PFC and RFC. Finally, consider a scheme (Case IV) in which an extra six marks are allotted for caste backwardness and an extra three marks for poverty: both caste and economic status are seen as grounds for preferential treatment. In this situation, the effective marks of PBC, RBC, PFC and RFC will be, respectively, 79 (six extra marks for caste backwardness and three extra marks for the condition of poverty), 87 (six extra marks for caste backwardness), 86 (three extra marks for poverty) and 85 (no extra marks at all), and the selected candidates will be RBC and PFC. These details are conveniently summarized in the table below. (Notice that the table reflects the judgement and the assumption we started out with.)

Selected Candidates under Alternative Schemes of Compensatory Discrimination

Scheme of compensatory discrimination	'Effective' marks of poor backward caste candidate (PBC)	'Effective' marks of rich backward caste candidate (RBC)	'Effective' marks of poor forward caste candidate (PFC)	'Effective' marks of rich forward caste candidate (RFC)	Qualifying mark	Selected candidates
I	70	81	83	85	80	PFC, RFC
II	76	87	83	85	80	RBC, RFC
III	76	81	83	85	80	PFC, RFC
IV	79	87	86	85	80	RBC, PFC

The Four Alternative Schemes

Let us consider each of the schemes of compensatory discrimination in turn. Scheme I, which does not allow for any group-related preferential treatment whatever, is the sort of scheme that would be favoured by an undiluted belief in the virtues of meritocracy: notice that it is the two members of the forward caste who are selected under this scheme. No doubt there are large numbers of individuals—of predictable caste and class affiliations—who would approve of Scheme I. We shall, however, take the view that Scheme I does not belong in any reasonable discourse on social justice: it is a bit late in the day to deny, for instance, the historical and contemporary reality of the disadvantages imposed by the caste system.

An acknowledgement of this reality is compatible with a scheme of compensatory discrimination such as Scheme II, which endorses preferential treatment in the event of caste disadvantage. For the example we have considered, the candidates who are selected under this scheme are RBC and RFC. Given a certain perspective, this outcome is unfair to PFC: the poor, forward caste person is seen as having been forced to lose out unjustly to the rich, backward caste person. This perception plays an important role in upholding the 'creamy layer principle', which underlies Scheme III.

Notice that the distribution of 'effective' marks under Scheme III is different from what it is under Scheme I: in particular, PBC's effective marks are higher (at 76) in Scheme III than in Scheme I (at 70), and this fact can serve as a basis for upholding the 'justice' of the scheme. For all practical purposes, however, neither of the backward caste candidates is helped by Scheme III: PBC's 'raw' marks are too low to be aided by the preferential treatment to which he is eligible, and RBC, by virtue of being rich enough to belong to the 'creamy layer', is not eligible for caste-based preferential treatment at all. The outcome of Scheme III is that it is the two forward caste candidates that are selected. *This outcome is identical to the one corresponding to Scheme I: consequentially, it makes no difference whether it is Scheme III that is implemented or a scheme that does not allow for any caste-related preferential treatment.*

In judging the merit of any principle of social justice, there is a strong case for being guided (even if not exclusively) by consequentialist considerations. By this reckoning, the 'creamy layer principle' underlying Scheme III puts up a pretty poor showing. If the grievance with the Scheme II outcome is that the poor, forward caste candidate has not been adequately compensated for his disadvantaged economic status, then that grievance is badly served by invoking the 'creamy layer principle': the solution does not reside in asserting that the social and educational disadvantage of a backward caste group is obliterated at some (sufficiently high) level of income. Assuming there is merit in the grievance just described, a more rational approach to the problem would consist in basing preferential treatment on grounds of both caste *and* economic status. This, precisely, is the view that underlies Scheme IV. Under this scheme, the outcome is that the selected candidates are RBC and PFC. Notice that, of the two rich candidates RBC and RFC, Scheme IV favours the candidate disadvantaged by caste; and of the two forward caste candidates PFC and RFC, Scheme IV favours the candidate disadvantaged by poverty. This, one would imagine, is as it should be: the outcome respects the 'other things equal' clause in the arbitration of competing claims. The grievance with the Scheme II outcome, reviewed earlier, is rectified under Scheme IV: the poor, forward caste person is now selected. We are also now enabled to see that the sense of PFC having been forced to lose out to RBC under Scheme II is a misguided one: it is more meaningful to see PFC as having lost out to RFC, an aberration that is corrected under Scheme IV, which avoids also the aberration, under Scheme III, of having RBC lose out to RFC.

The outcome under Scheme III has the further effect of widening the gulf between the backward and the forward castes. In course of time, the need for preferential treatment to the backward castes would reassert itself with vehemence. When this need is sought to be addressed, a so-called 'creamy layer' of the backward caste may be expected to manifest itself again. If this calls forth a proscription of preferential treatment to the rich among the backward caste, then one would have to fall back once more on a Scheme III mechanism of compensatory discrimination. One can look forward to a perpetual oscillation between Schemes II and III. The need for caste-based preferential treatment will then be never-ending. And this would be a consequence of disregarding a dictum (here paraphrased) of B.R. Ambedkar's: that one has to have preferential treatment in order to annihilate preferential treatment. It is at least a little ironical that the 'creamy layer principle' is often invoked alongside an impatient demand for a time-bound cessation of caste-based preferential treatment, when precisely this principle may be expected to grant preferential treatment an indefinite lease of life. And quite apart from this, one would imagine that an elementary level of social maturity, combined with a sense of proportion, would dictate vastly more urgent deadlines for a cessation of caste atrocities than for a cessation of the phenomenon of reservation.

Professed and Real Rationales

There is a real and a professed rationale for the 'creamy layer principle', the former of which has been reviewed above (and found seriously wanting). A professed rationale often held out is based on a concern for a fairer distribution *within* the backward caste group. This rationale, when it is not insincere, is certainly paternalistic and condescending. First, the issue of group-related preferential treatment is, by its very nature, an issue of social justice addressed to the question of *inter*-group equality, not *intra*-group equality. As such, the concern should essentially be with group averages of relevant indicators of well-being, not with questions of how the total is distributed within any group. For, no matter how distributed, if the average for a currently disadvantaged group rises sufficiently over time, then that should be a signal for moving the group out of the ambit of preferential treatment. (Indeed, for the average to rise over time, any presently observed 'layer' would have to thicken with time.) Notice that the discourse is about including *groups* within, or excluding *groups* from, the scope of preferential treatment, and not about including or excluding *individuals* within particular groups. On the other hand, if it is fair to import considerations of within-group inequality into the discourse, then there is a strong case for being even-handed in the matter—indeed, the more so because it is well known that the intra-group distribution of resources is more unequal among the forward than the backward castes. The forward caste concern for inequality within the backward caste group is a fit candidate for the advice: 'Physician, heal thyself.' (A less classically restrained injunction would be the American colloquialism: 'Mind yer bizness.')

A large part of the appeal of the 'creamy layer principle' resides in the principle's nomenclature. The image of overweight, indolent, dishonest and undeserving elements among the backward castes which the 'creamy layer' appellation conjures up is one which inhibits the need for a more detailed scrutiny of the principle as an acceptable tenet of social justice. Such a slightly more careful examination suggests that the principle is a misguided one from both logical and sociological perspectives.

A RESPONSE TO PROFESSORS K. SUNDARAM AND K. RAVI SRINIVAS

Introduction

I am grateful to Professor Sundaram (2007) and Professor Ravi Srinivas (2007) for having taken the trouble of commenting on my article. In what follows, I shall try to respond to their criticisms as well as I am able. Given constraints on space, I shall mainly address Sundaram's discussion, which strikes me as being more straightforwardly directed at my article, while making references, where relevant, to Ravi Srinivas' comments.

I believe Sundaram's comment can be seen in the light of three major points he makes. First, he suggests that my argument is located in the format of a 'handicap race' rather than in one of a 'pre-assigned quota', which latter is what is relevant to the context of discussion. (This also is a point made by Ravi Srinivas.) Second, he suggests that skimming off the creamy layer among the backward caste group need not necessarily compromise the extent of backward caste representation in aggregate educational attainment. Third, he suggests that, contrary to my assertion, within-group inequality, at least in the matter of certain aspects of educational achievement, is more pronounced for the backward caste than for the forward caste. I address each of these points in turn.

'Handicap Race' versus 'Pre-assigned Quota'

As I had tried to indicate in my article, my objective was to examine some possible implications of the creamy layer prescription for between-group equality, at a certain abstract level of the underlying principle involved. I had also warned that my approach was not intended to encompass nuance, nor complexity, nor a literal representation of reality. The idea was simply to convey (and to convey simply) the essential logic of a certain line of reasoning. Having said this, I believe it should be possible, at the expense of a little incremental complexity, to reformulate my 'handicap race' argument into a corresponding 'pre-assigned quota' argument.

Imagine, as before, that there are two castes (backward and forward: BC and FC, respectively) and two economic classes (poor and rich: P and R, respectively). Suppose four seats are available for admission to a professional college, and that there are 10 candidates competing for the seats. Of these, let us suppose that three candidates are PBC, three RBC, two PFC and two RFC. The distribution of marks is: 70 for each of the three PBC candidates, 76 for each of the three RBC candidates, 83 for each of the two PFC candidates and 85 for each of the two RFC candidates.

In the absence of any quota provision for those that may be perceived to constitute disadvantaged groups, and assuming a qualifying mark of 82 (Case I), the selected candidates will be the two RFCs and the two PFCs. Suppose now that a 50 per cent quota is reserved for the backward caste, with a qualifying mark of 75 for the reserved category and one of 82 for the open category (Case II). Then, the selected candidates will be the two RFCs and any two of the three RBCs. Next, suppose we have a scheme of 50 per cent reservation, with a qualifying mark of 75, for backward caste persons, but provided only that they are also poor, and a qualifying mark of 82 for the open category (Case III). Then, the caste quota will be of no avail to the three PBC candidates because of their low marks, while the three RBC individuals, because of their 'creamy layer' status, will have to compete in the open category, where they will lose out to the two RFC and the two PFC candidates. Finally, consider a scheme (Scheme IV) in which 50 per cent of the seats are reserved for caste backwardness, with a qualifying mark of 75, and 25 per cent are reserved for economic backwardness (irrespective of caste affiliation), with a qualifying mark of 80, while the qualifying mark in the open category is 82: in this case, and given the specific, assumed distribution of marks across the castes and the classes, two of the three RBC candidates will be selected under the 'caste quota', one of the two PFC candidates will be selected under the 'poverty quota' and one of the two RFC candidates will be selected in the open category.

In Cases I and III, the backward caste candidates find no representation in the set of selected persons (the 'creamy layer' criterion is consequentially equivalent to the no–compensatory-discrimination outcome) and Schemes II and IV ensure that 50 per cent of the selected candidates belong to the backward caste, with Scheme IV ensuring that the open category seats are not confined to the rich among the forward caste. These 'pre-assigned quota' outcomes are very similar to their original 'handicap race' counterparts dealt with in my article.

I might as well state here, explicitly, that I have carefully selected the numbers required to yield the above results. The example I have dealt with was intended to illustrate the proposition that implementation of the creamy layer principle could exacerbate caste disparities in access to education. If, in line with Ravi Srinivas' complaint, this is an exercise in tautology, I am afraid there is no help for it. An example explicitly intended to illustrate a certain proposition must presumably end up illustrating it. I would imagine this is in the nature of things. Arising from which, if there is little to be said for making a virtue of necessity, then there is equally little to be said for making a vice of necessity.

The Creamy Layer Criterion and Backward Caste Representation

The second point which Sundaram makes is grounded in useful empirical work. (Ravi Srinivas complains that I myself have not offered any findings from empirical research. Apart from the fact that I did not make any claims to the contrary, all I can say is that I am very happy for him, or anyone else, to engage in the requisite empirical research.) The import of Sundaram's data-based analysis can be reformulated in the following simple terms. Let Q stand for the number of seats allotted to the backward caste under a quota reservation system and let E be the number of eligible candidates from the backward caste. One of the 'essentially empirical questions' which Sundaram suggests should be addressed in assessing whether the implementation of a creamy layer criterion could adversely affect backward caste representation in admissions, is that of the relative magnitudes of Q and E. If E is greater than Q, then—Sundaram seems to infer—the basis for the apprehension just mentioned is removed. Let us suppose that E is indeed greater than Q and let D be the (positive) difference between E and Q. Further, let CL be the size of the identified 'creamy layer'. The positivity of D is just one of the empirical questions that need to be checked. Another important question is the size of CL. If CL is greater than D, then the basis for the apprehension outlined earlier is *not* removed.

Why should one object to implementation of a creamy layer criterion if CL $\leq D$? This begs a prior question: why *have* a creamy layer criterion at all? Once the legitimacy of the principle is acknowledged, it is a matter of the camel's head in the tent. The debate will quickly shift to where the size of CL should be pitched. One should be possessed of an uncommonly large stock of naivety to believe that the aggressive, broomstick-wielding votaries of the creamy layer principle will have any use for that principle if CL is identified in such a way that CL $\leq D$. Empirical information is provided not only in columns of data in Census or NSSO publications, but on the streets outside as well! But apart from instrumental reasons, there are also intrinsic ones for treading warily in the presence of the creamy layer principle.

I would like to reiterate the point made in my article—that affirmative action relates to questions of inter-group, not intra-group, equality. Restricting the creamy layer principle to cases in which CL ≤ D can only be motivated by a pure concern for within-group equality among members of the backward caste. It is one thing to express this concern in exhortatory terms, but another to seek legislative endorsement for it; also, there is a strong case for permitting these concerns to emerge more 'organically' from within the backward caste community itself. Second, if concerns of within-group equality must be imported into the discourse, why restrict these concerns only to the backward caste? Professor Sundaram does seem to endorse a more even-handed approach to the issue of intra-group equality when he says: '...even as one accepts the need to address inequalities in access to higher education among the forward castes by substantially expanding the availability to them of means-based scholarships, there is a strong case for excluding the "creamy layer" of the backward castes in a quota regime'. Why is the redress of forward caste inequality located in 'substantially expanding the availability of means-based scholarships', while the redress of backward caste inequality is located in skimming off the creamy layer? Notice that the eligibility criterion, in terms of qualifying marks, would become more stringent for the backward caste creamy layer members if they were graduated out of the quota ambit into the open category. A more consistent approach would be to either (a) simply substantially expand the availability of means-based scholarships to the more disadvantaged members of the backward caste; or (b) implement a creamy layer criterion (subject to CL ≤ D) for the backward caste and implement a similar equality-preferring scheme of differentially higher qualifying marks for the forward caste creamy layer. One has to wonder if all the complexity of backward and forward caste creamy layer identification, together with the problem of coming up with a satisfactory scheme of differentiated eligibility criteria, would indeed be worth the trouble.

There is no question of refusing to acknowledge that some defendants of the creamy layer principle are motivated by a pure concern for within-group backward caste equality (though, as argued above, it is not clear that implementation of a creamy layer criterion is the appropriate solution to their problem). Having said this, I would reiterate a point made in my earlier article: that, often enough, there is a difference between the real and professed reasons for favouring the creamy layer principle. It is not even always evident that votaries of the principle are, in fact, themselves self-consciously aware of the difference. In this connection, I shall confine myself to observing briefly that while Ravi Srinivas' commentary begins on a note of concern for equality within the backward caste group, it ends on a note of grievance on behalf of the forward caste group.

Backward and Forward Caste within-group Inequality

Finally, I address Professor Sundaram's third point on the empirical validity of greater within-group inequality in the distribution of resources for the forward than for the backward caste. I am afraid there is a straightforward misunderstanding here. I did not say that there is greater inequality in the distribution of educational attainment in the forward caste group than in the backward caste group—I could not have, for a reason which I will discuss in the next paragraph. What I did say is: '…if it is fair to import considerations of within-group inequality into the discourse, then there is a strong case for being even-handed in the matter—indeed, the more so because it is well known that the intra-group distribution of resources is more unequal among the forward than the backward castes'. For instance, data in the 1991–92 NSS survey on *Assets and Liabilities of Rural and Urban Households* suggest that at the all India level, in each of the rural and urban areas, both the Gini and the Theil indices of inequality in the distribution of household assets were lower for the scheduled caste and tribe group than for the non-scheduled caste and tribe group. Yet, there is little evidence of prescriptions for within-group redistribution of assets among the forward caste group—which marks a strong contrast from the strangely solicitous concern for inequality in the distribution of educational attainment within the backward caste group. In any event, and for the point I was stressing, it suffices that there be a finite level of inequality in the distribution of resources among the forward caste; it is not necessary that this level be higher than what it is for the backward caste.

Insofar as the within-group distribution of educational attainment is concerned, one should expect, at the outset, that the Gini coefficient of inequality will be higher for the backward than for the forward caste, and a reverse claim would be *a priori* indefensible. The reason for this is discussed in what follows. When, for example, we speak of those with or without a higher secondary certificate, we are speaking of a binary variable that takes the value 0 for those who are deprived, and the value 1 for those who are not deprived. For a population of size n, if the mean of the distribution under review is m, and if n is sufficiently large, the Gini coefficient G can be approximated by the expression $1 - (2/n^2m)\sum_{i=1}^{n}$ $(n + 1 - i)x_i$, where x_i is the ith *poorest* person's resource level. If x_i is interpreted as the ith poorest person's headcount ratio of access to a given state of educational achievement, then x_i is either 0 or 1, and it is very easy to verify that G is simply H, where H is the proportion of the population without access to the educational achievement in question. One must expect H—and therefore G—to be lower for the forward than for the backward caste group. For the distribution of a binary (0–1)-valued variable, it just so happens that G (an index of disparity) coincides with H (an index of deprivation): the group with lower inequality is simply the less deprived group. In such a situation, within-group inequality is just a manifestation of group poverty.

The above considerations are relevant for Sundaram's finding that 'in respect of Urban youth in the 17–25 age-group, relative to the distribution of population of each social group across expenditure groups defining quintiles of the total urban population, *the distribution of population with a Higher Secondary Certificate or of those currently attending Under-graduate courses or of those with a 'Graduate and Above' level of completed education, is in fact more unequal among the backward castes than among the forward castes*' (emphasis in original). I take it that the 'Gini coefficients' reported in his table relate to the caste-wise distribution of educational attainment across *expenditure* groups; and if this is so, the result he obtains is not surprising in a situation, as is generally the case, where educational attainment is an increasing function of income.

For example, let $(x_1, \ldots, x_{10})$ be a 10-vector of income levels arranged in ascending order, namely $x_1 < x_2 < \ldots < x_{10}$. If the headcount ratio H of, say, failure to enter college, is 70 per cent (call this Case A), it is likely that the college entrants are persons 8, 9 and 10. If the headcount ratio declines to 50 per cent (call this Case B), the entrants would be likely to be persons 6, 7, 8, 9 and 10. As deprivation declines, the concentration of educational attainment among the richer individuals would tend to get diluted. Since deprivation in the forward caste is lower than in the backward caste, there is less income-related concentration of educational achievement in the former than in the latter.

Interestingly, this suggests that there could be two ways of diluting concentration. Going back to Case A, let us imagine that it describes the backward caste distribution in a situation where there is a 30 per cent quota and all of it has been 'cornered' by the richest individuals (8, 9, and 10). One could now aim at one of two stratagems. First, one could retain H at 0.7 and arrange— by, say, skimming off the creamy layer (persons 9 and 10)—for persons 6, 7, and 8 to enter college. Alternatively, one could seek to reduce the educational deprivation rate from 0.7 to 0.5, and reduce concentration by transiting from Case A to Case B. The latter stratagem, surely, is preferable. One obvious means to this end would be to *increase the size of the quota* (from 30 per cent to 50 per cent)—a possible prescription that flows out of Sundaram's finding. Somehow, I get the feeling that Sundaram may not endorse the prescription!

Concluding Observations

In the end, it is vitally important that positions should be advanced, or defended, or rebutted, through recourse to logic and reasoning. But surely, a fine-grained sense of arithmetic is only aided by a sense of perspective as well. The latter should assist in recognizing that, in the matter of caste in India, there are rather more urgent issues of justice to contend with than resisting a perceived 'unfairness' in some particular arrangement of preferential treatment. In a very general way, such a recognition, informed as it would be by a little less flintiness and a little more generosity of spirit, can create the conditions for a vastly more productive discussion of issues relating to compensatory discrimination than appears now to be the case. I cannot hope to improve upon the sentiment expressed by my late and well-remembered friend S. Guhan, when he said:

> There can be constructive debate on these practical matters but what is of prior importance is to agree that philosophically and politically social discrimination in India has to be corrected through concrete measures for social justice. The process is bound to be painful, but we should accept the pain as the necessary concomitant of the maturation of our society and nation. (Guhan 2001)

References

Guhan, S. (2001), 'Social Discrimination and Caste Reservations' in S. Subramanian (ed.) *India's Development Experience: Selected Writings of S. Guhan*. Oxford University Press: Delhi.

Ravi Srinivas, K. (2007), 'Demystifying the Anti-Creamy Layer', *Economic and Political Weekly*, 42(5): 327–8.

Sundaram, K. (2007), '"Creamy Layer Principle": A Comment', *Economic and Political Weekly*, 42(5): 326–7.

PART II

Between Economics and Philosophy

10
Headcount Poverty Comparisons*

The most elementary, and also the most widely employed, means of assessing the extent of poverty in any society is to obtain a simple headcount of the poor. The poor are those whose incomes fall short of a stipulated poverty line. The commonest measure of poverty is the *headcount ratio*, H, which is the proportion of the poor in the total population. An alternative, and far less routinely used headcount index, is the *aggregate headcount*, A, which is the total absolute number of the poor. A problem for the measurement of poverty—and one which is only rarely acknowledged by professional economists—is that the headcount ratio and the aggregate headcount can provide contrary poverty rankings. For example, if in some initial time period 30 persons in a population of 100 are poor, while in a later time period 40 persons in a population of 200 are poor, then the headcount ratio *declines* from 30 per cent to 20 per cent, whereas the aggregate headcount *rises* from 30 persons to 40 persons. This type of problem is often encountered. For example, using a poverty line of 2.15 Purchasing Power Parity dollars per person per day, the global headcount ratio

* This essay appeared as paper 18 (November 2005) in the 'One-Pager' series of the United Nations Development Programme's International Policy Centre for Inclusive Growth, Brasilia, Brazil. It has been included in the *IPC-IG Collection of One-Pagers*, published by the UNDP's International Policy Centre for Inclusive Growth in September 2009 (Brasilia: Brazil).

has been estimated to have declined from 66.7 per cent in 1981 to 52.9 per cent in 1991, while over the same period, the global aggregate headcount has been estimated to have risen from 2,450 million to 2,735 million.[1]

A strong argument in favour of the headcount ratio over the aggregate headcount is that the former, unlike the latter, satisfies what one might call a '*Likelihood Principle*', which is the requirement that a poverty measure should convey some information about the probability of encountering a poor person in any given society. On the other hand, the aggregate headcount, unlike the headcount ratio, satisfies a principle called the '*Constituency Principle*'. This is a general principle of well-being comparisons formulated by the economist–philosopher John Broome, and it demands something like the following. If a given set of individuals has been identified as the only constituency which is of relevance in ascertaining the 'goodness' of a state of affairs, then the 'goodness' of alternative states of affairs should be compared only in terms of the interests of the identified constituency in the states under comparison. When we speak of poverty, it seems eminently reasonable to designate the *poor* population as the only relevant constituency for ascertaining the extent of poverty. And if this is the case, it follows that additions to either the incomes or the size of the non-poor population should be treated as wholly irrelevant information when it comes to making poverty comparisons.

It is easy to see that the headcount ratio, in contrast to the aggregate headcount, violates the constituency principle. Here is a simple example. Imagine an initial situation in which we have a two-person society, with the incomes of the two individuals being ₹1,000 and ₹3,000, respectively, and with the poverty line set at ₹2,000. It is clear that the headcount ratio for this society is 50 per cent. Suppose now that a person with an income of ₹3,000 joins this society. Then, the headcount ratio will decline to 33.33 per cent. With the addition of a third person with an income of ₹3,000, the headcount ratio will decline further to 25 per cent. Add one more person whose income is ₹3,000, and the headcount ratio will come down to 20 per cent. And so on. If we simply keep inflating the size of the non-poor population, before long we will be in a position to claim that we have—by measuring poverty in terms of the headcount ratio—almost completely eradicated poverty, even though precisely *nothing* has been done to redress the poverty of the only person who represents the constituency of the poor in the society under review.

So where does this leave us? The headcount ratio H satisfies the likelihood principle and violates the constituency principle, while the aggregate headcount A satisfies the constituency principle and violates the likelihood principle. Leaving poverty judgements entirely up to either H or A could be a risky proposition. This suggests the possible wisdom of a 'compromise solution', whereby we look at both H and A, in a bid to avoid the extreme judgement of either principle in isolation. In this note, I only pose the problem, without considering solutions for it, simply in order to underline the fact that the problem has rather serious conceptual and practical implications for the measurement and comparison of poverty (see Subramanian 2002; Chakravarty et al. 2006).

End Note

1. This is a liberal version of the World Bank's poverty line using 1993 as the base year. See Martin Ravallion's contribution to the IPC's *In Focus* issue titled 'Dollar a Day, How Much Does It Say?' (September 2004).

References

Chakravarty, S., S.R. Kanbur, and D. Mukherji. (2006), 'Population Growth and Poverty Measurement', *Social Choice and Welfare*, 26(3): 471–83.

Subramanian, S. (2002), 'Counting the Poor: An Elementary Difficulty in the Measurement of Poverty', *Economics and Philosophy*, 18(2): 277–85.

11
Thinking Through Justice*

The Book and This Review

Amartya Sen's book on justice is a remarkable intellectual achievement of analytical skill, scholarship, and insight. It both owes much to, and departs from, the approach and content of its illustrious predecessor, John Rawls' *A Theory of Justice*. The present piece is an extended review of *The Idea of Justice*, which offers a capsule précis of Rawls' earlier work on justice, a fairly detailed summary of Sen's own concerns in *The Idea of Justice*, some critical observations on the book, and an invitation to the reader to view Rawls' and Sen's contributions as affording contrasting, but also valuably complementary perspectives, on the notion of justice.

The book's subject is one of those matters on which nearly everybody has an opinion. Most of us believe we know what justice is, not least in the sense of its being the *opposite* of 'injustice'. After all, it is rather easier to recognize when injustice is experienced than it is to actually define, or describe, or elaborate on, the notion of justice, as such. Any such elaboration, it is useful to register at the very outset, must be expected to differ distinctively from the form and content of everyday discourses on justice. The

*This essay was originally published as a review article of Amartya Sen's (2009) *The Idea of Justice*. [Allen Lane (an imprint of Penguin Books), pp. xix + 468.] It was published as: 'Thinking Through Justice' (2010), *Economic and Political Weekly*, 45(19): 33–42.

latter are concerned with specific passions and interests; with particular historical conjunctures; with immediate political considerations; and with hard pragmatic questions of strategy that must be deployed to secure redress for injustice or to ensure the protection and preservation of justice within well-defined projects that could be as diverse in their engagement and aspirations as class struggle, caste emancipation, national sovereignty, environmental conservation or gender equity.

It is unlikely that broadly conceived philosophical treatises on justice—which address general principles rather than particular applications—will afford social revolutionaries or nationalists or environmentalists or feminists with proximate, concrete and detailed direction on justice-related questions with regard to their respective and specialized projects. Those that would nevertheless insist on such immediate relevance, applicability, and guidance as necessary conditions for acceptability are bound to find books in the Sen genre to be disappointing. I state this in a factual, not evaluative, spirit. It is useful then—and fair, I think—to assess a book such as Sen's in terms of considerations that arise from within the limits of its jurisdiction, while recognizing that these limits, though very extensive from one perspective, might nevertheless be too constraining, from another, to be of interest to readers of certain persuasions and expectations. It is therefore just as well to point out that neither the book nor this review can be of much appeal for such readers. I state this without prejudice to either the book or the category of readers I have mentioned.

Judged on its own terms, however, I believe that a book such as Sen's, which aims to present a responsible, coherent and deliberative account of the notion of justice and its constitutive parts, reflects a hugely difficult undertaking. It is doubly difficult to perform this task in a manner which (a) preserves the rigour of careful thinking, (b) is not guilty of talking down to the listener from a height, and yet (c) succeeds in including all who are willing to listen within the fold of a complex but nevertheless lucid and accessible discourse. It is this feat of a general and overarching treatment of the subject—truly a case of Justice for All—that Amartya Sen pulls off in his *Idea of Justice*. The book is as remarkable for its scholarship and analytical acuity as it is relaxed and engaging in its exposition of difficult concepts. The latter is marked by the author's persistent resort to anecdotes, quotations, examples from history, literary embellishments, chattiness, and even gossip (what did Pierre de Fermat write to Rene Descartes and what was Descartes' reaction?). This book is the product of a lifetime's engagement with its subject. It is an extraordinary piece of work.

In what follows, I shall try and summarize, insofar as I am able, some of Sen's principal concerns in this book. I shall then raise certain questions that strike me as being pertinent, before concluding. (In respect of these questions, I can only hope that my teacher will be as tolerant now as he was over 30 years ago in the classroom, allowing for the possibility that not all of us grow older *and* wiser.) By way of a preliminary exercise, though, I shall offer an encapsulated version of the work of John Rawls on justice. This is important, because, first, it is difficult to conduct any discussion of justice in moral and political philosophy without regard to Rawls' work; and, second, Rawls—to whose memory *The Idea of Justice* has been dedicated—has had a profound effect on Sen, at least as much in the matter of where and how Sen *dis*agrees with him as in the matter of where and how Sen agrees.

Rawls

In this very brief background discussion, I shall deal only with two specifically important contributions of Rawls' to the subject of justice. It is a matter of wide agreement that among the most significant and influential of contemporary treatments of the idea of justice is Rawls' (1971) book *A Theory of Justice*. While this work is seen as dealing with the requirements of 'domestic' justice, Rawls' (1999) book *The Law of Peoples* deals with the requirements of 'international' justice.

Rawls has been much concerned with a particular notion of justice—that of 'justice as fairness', a manifestation of which he sees as residing in the outcome of a certain highly imaginative bargaining process, aimed at realizing a just society and conducted in a fictive place of the mind he calls the 'original position'. In *A Theory of Justice*, Rawls invites us to engage in a thought experiment involving the conjuring up of a primordial situation called the 'original position'. In this original position, the actual citizens of a society are imagined to be represented, one-for-one, by a group of deliberators acting in the interests of their clients, but behind a hypothetical 'veil of ignorance' which ensures that the deliberators are ignorant of any and all relevant features that may characterize their clients in the 'real world'. This 'representational device' of Rawls' is intended to secure those features of impartiality and objectivity which it would be natural to see as informing the notion of justice as fairness. What sort of social compact might the deliberators in the original position arrive at?

In the assumed conditions under which the deliberators bargain a social contract, Rawls argues that a public criterion of justice, involving two principles—the liberty principle and the difference principle—will emerge. Rawls' first principle of justice—required to hold foundationally prior to all else—demands that each person is to have an equal right to the most widespread liberty compatible with a like liberty for all. The second principle—the celebrated difference principle—emphasizes the primacy of maximizing the advantage (in terms of an index of primary goods, which includes such things as incomes, wealth, opportunities and the social bases of self-respect) of the worst-off person: specifically, 'social and economic inequalities are to be arranged so that they are both (a) to the greatest benefit of the least advantaged and (b) attached to offices and positions open to all under conditions of fair equality of opportunity' (Rawls 1971: 83). To secure 'the greatest benefit of the least advantaged' is a matter of 'maximizing the minimum': hence the often-employed characterization of Rawls' contribution in terms of the so-called 'maximin principle' of justice. A just society is one which will address itself to the creation, design and promotion of social institutions (the 'background structure') which will advance the cause of the criterion of public justice encompassing the twin principles just mentioned.

In *The Law of Peoples*, intended to deal with the issue of international justice, Rawls effects some significant departures from the
approach to domestic justice considered in *A Theory of Justice*. Most
saliently, the deliberators in the original position are now conceived of as representing *peoples*, rather than *persons*. Parties to the
deliberation are confined to those peoples that Rawls calls 'liberal
peoples' and 'decent peoples'. The former are committed to political liberalism in the internal structure of their society, whereas the
latter reflect some shortfalls from a full commitment to political
liberalism and yet display the promise, in the face of toleration and
inclusion, of eventual transformation into well-ordered societies.
Wholly illiberal and oppressive societies are kept out of the ambit
of the deliberations in the original position. Unlike in the approach
to domestic justice, the outcome of the bargaining process underlying international justice is seen as securing not a public criterion
of social justice (as enshrined in the liberty and difference principles), but as leading to the direct specification of some eight rules
which are supposed to govern the conduct of states in their inter-
actions with one another—rules relating, for instance, to compliance with treaties, with human rights, with non-intervention, with
mutual aid and so on. As pointed out by Thomas Pogge (2004),
in the transition from domestic to international justice, the shift
in emphasis from persons to peoples effectively marks a shift away
from the insistence, in a *Theory of Justice*, on normative individualism. We shall revisit these themes at a later point in the essay. What
we need to do now is to return, from this (necessary) digression
into Rawls, to Sen's *Idea of Justice*.

Transcendental Institutionalism and Social Realization

In seeking to summarize Sen's book, I shall resort to somewhat
drastic abbreviation and simplification. The job does occasion me
a guilty conscience but not one which is irredeemably troubled,
thanks to the license which Sen himself affords (on p. 53), when

he says: '...every summary is ultimately an act of barbarism....' One could commence the present act of barbarism by noting that Sen characterizes the Rawlsian approach—and similar, typically 'contractarian', approaches—to justice as belonging to the mould of 'transcendental institutionalism'. Such approaches are transcendental in the sense of being informed by the demands of perfect justice, as reflected in some unique public criterion of justice. They are geared towards institutionalism in the sense of demanding only that the right 'background structure' be put in place, which is the requirement of the design and promotion of such institutions as will further the cause of the public criterion of justice. Often enough, this institutional emphasis is accompanied by idealized specifications of human behaviour on the part of agents in the real world, behaviour that exhibits compliance with just procedures and a refusal to yield to the temptation of reneging on promises that it may no longer be in one's best interests to keep.

Sen contrasts such a perspective with an alternative approach to conceptualizing justice, one which emphasizes the virtue of 'social realization'. The concern here is not (or at least not only) with institutional arrangements geared to the demands of justice, but with a reckoning of how people's lives actually go, with the issue of assessing justice in terms of the real achievements and accomplishments of real agents in alternative states of affairs. In this view, there is a break from the 'transcendental' obsession of identifying one superlative and unsurpassed expression of justice, which yields place to the more modest, but also more realistic and productive perspective of the 'comparative' approach, whereby one can promote the cause of a dispensation which is more just than the *status quo ante* without having to specify the most just one. The contrast between 'transcendental institutionalism' and 'social realization' permits Sen to effect a number of related distinctions and contrasts, as between deontological and consequence-sensitive moral reasoning, as between processes and outcomes, and as between *niti* and *nyaya* (the jurisprudential notions of justice in classical Sanskrit corresponding, roughly, to procedural propriety and substantively consummated right, respectively).

Social Choice Theory and the Comparative Perspective

Sen finds the discipline of social choice theory (whose greatest modern exponent has been Kenneth Arrow (1963) of Stanford University) very congenial to the task of addressing issues of justice. For one thing, social choice is concerned with ranking sets of alternatives which are typically taken to be 'social states'—what Arrow characterizes as complete descriptions of society, including every individual's position in it. This already fits in nicely with Sen's requirement that justice be concerned with 'social realizations'. Further, the ranking of social states fits in nicely with the 'comparative perspective' that Sen advocates. The 'transcendental' approach, by contrast, does not entail the comparative approach; the former is neither necessary nor sufficient for the latter. Within the framework of social choice, the identification of a 'best' state of affairs is neither invariably feasible nor desirable. Pair-wise comparisons of social states do not necessarily lead to the emergence of an identifiably best (set) of alternative(s), unless the binary preference relation that is pressed into service should be an ordering defined over a finite set of alternatives. Sen regards the property of 'completeness' of a binary relation R (the property that for any pair of alternatives x and y one *should* be able to pronounce that either xRy or yRx is true) to be an over-praised virtue. For long, Sen has maintained that *forcing* comparability when it is not warranted can be misleading and unproductive (we do not *have* to be able to say—to take one example—that for every conceivable pair of income distributions, one distribution is at least as unequal as the other). Social choice theory can live with such partial comparisons, and yet deliver substantial insights into matters of justice, by facilitating (wherever possible) a ranking of social realizations that is accommodated within the framework of the comparative perspective.

Social choice theory, it is clear, is more closely allied in spirit to the *nyaya* (social realization oriented) than the *niti* (conduct/process/protocol oriented) conception of justice, as reflected in the distinction between evaluating states of affairs on the one hand

and evaluating matters related to obligation, onus, or duty on the other. A classic version of the consequentialist vs. deontological lines of moral reasoning which Sen discusses is the mirrored debate between Krishna and Arjuna in the *Bhagavadgita*. While displaying an overall commitment to *nyaya*, Sen is careful also to warn that consequentialism, or sensitivity to the consequences of actions, must not be reduced to the evaluation of 'cumulative outcomes'. What ought to matter, rather, are 'comprehensive outcomes', which allow room for a consideration of agency, responsibility, personal relations, and processes.

The Informational Focus of Social Realization: The Space of Capabilities

If the favoured conception of justice is one that engages with social realizations—with the concern regarding how people's lives go—then it must address the question of informational focus, the question of the domain or space in which individual human advantage is most meaningfully reckoned. Economists, typically, have been concerned with income (as reflected in their preoccupation with growth in per capita GNP) as the space most meriting attention; Bentham-ites have been concerned with the space of utilities; Rawlsians with primary goods; and 'resourcists' in general, with 'resources' in general. Sen's distinctive contribution to justice discourse—as also that of the philosopher Martha Nussbaum (2000)—has been the invocation of the space of *human capabilities*. The capabilities Sen refers to are the capabilities to function, a functioning being a state of being or doing. A functioning bundle is a collection of specific functionings, and could, in some specific instance, be a more or less precise description of an individual's nutritional status, her mobility status, her literacy status, her housing status, and her status in respect of what Adam Smith called the ability to appear in public without shame (a functioning whose value Sen has for long championed). A person's capability set is the set of all functioning bundles actually available to her—a description of those various alternative combinations of being and doing which she can attain to. As such, and in a somewhat straightforward sense, a person's capability reflects her substantive freedom to achieve those functionings that she values and has reason to value.

As has been mentioned earlier, *The Idea of Justice* reflects its author's engagement with certain issues over a long prior period of time. Sen's preoccupation with the 'capability approach' was presaged at least as far back in time as 1973 when his *On Economic Inequality* (1973) appeared. In that book, and subsequently, in his Tanner Lecture 'Equality of What?' (1980), he addressed the issue of the space in which inequality is most meaningfully assessed, given his understanding that all worthwhile moral theories are concerned with advancing the cause of equality in *some* space. Consider the case of an able-bodied person and a physically handicapped one: income-egalitarians would distribute income equally between the two individuals, and resource-egalitarians would resort to an equal distribution of resources, as would Rawlsians (to the extent that primary goods are resources, broadly conceived). In each case, an equal distribution would leave unaddressed the special and differential need of the physically handicapped person, because the handicapped individual would typically need more resources than the able-bodied one. The problem would be a good deal worse under the utilitarian prescription: if individual utility is an increasing function of income subject to diminishing increments, and the handicapped person's utility is lower than that of the able-bodied individual for every level of income, then the utilitarian formula of maximizing the sum total of individual utilities, entailing the equalization of marginal utilities, would result in awarding a larger share of the income to the able-bodied person, for he is the more efficient pleasure-machine. If human need makes a compelling impression upon our moral disposition towards distributional questions, then there would be a case for us to push in the direction of capability-equality.

Sen's emphasis on capabilities should also have (but regrettably has not) had a profound impact on the conceptualization and measurement of money-metric poverty. The 'identification' problem in the measurement of income poverty has to do with specifying a level of income—the poverty line—intended to separate the poor from the non-poor segments of a population. The 'aggregation' problem is concerned with coming up with an appropriate index of poverty on the basis of information on the underlying income distribution and the poverty line. In comparing alternative distributions in terms of poverty, it is clear that the standard for judging poverty should be invariant. In what space should we seek this invariance? Sen, in a paper dating back to 1983, was very clear on the answer. Recognizing that interpersonal variations in the ability to convert resources into income are an ineradicable fact of life, he pointed out that what we ought to be concerned about is invariance in the space of capabilities (or, more accurately, perhaps, functionings). Hence his contention that poverty should be specified absolutely in the space of functionings but (for the reason that not everybody converts incomes into functionings at the same rate) relatively in the space of incomes and resources. The capability perspective has also provided a basis for the exploration of direct assessments of poverty in functioning space through procedures aimed at measuring multidimensional (non-income) deprivation.

Liberty, Equality, and Justice

Liberty and equality, as we have seen earlier, are integral aspects of the Rawlsian conception of justice. The capability perspective also, in the light of the preceding discussion, emphasizes the importance of both freedom and equality in any overall assessment of the demands of justice. Sen discusses both the 'opportunity' and the 'process' aspects of freedom. The view of freedom stressed here is the 'positive freedom' view, one which is concerned with the actual capability of an individual to be or do this or that rather than only with his ability to pursue his desired ends in his protected personal sphere without hindrance or restraint. The latter, relatively 'negative', view of freedom is traditionally what is called 'liberty'. For Sen, as for Rawls, liberty is a prized social virtue, though Sen, unlike Rawls, does not accord lexical priority to liberty above all else. Even so, it is Sen who imported the language of libertarian rights into formal social choice theory through a small and piquant paper titled 'The Impossibility of a Paretian Liberal' (1970) which has succeeded in spawning an immense and often technically dense subsequent literature. This paper of Sen's is a prime example of his long-standing critique of 'welfarist' ways of thinking, with their exclusive focus on collective judgements that are required to be based solely on information pertaining to ordinal and interpersonally non-comparable individual utilities. In particular, Sen sought to demonstrate that the 'efficiency' property of Pareto optimality—a key concept in welfare economics and generally believed to be a hallmark of personal liberty—could actually turn out to be incompatible with a plausible formulation of a principle of liberty.

In the matter of equality, and wherever its demands are clear and uncontroversial (which, one supposes, would be the case under the operation of an 'everything else remaining the same' clause), Sen—as we have seen—favours capability equality. He is careful to underline though that justice does not invariably demand capability equality—partly because capability is not always the only dimension that matters and partly because equality is not always the only social virtue that matters.

Reasoning and Justice

The 'social realization' perspective thus affords a broadly useful mechanism—the reckoning of advantage in capability space—for ranking the justice content of alternative states of affairs within a framework of comparative judgement. This still leaves unanswered a number of questions: what are the capabilities that matter? How should they be weighed against one another? What considerations should guide the interpersonal aggregation of capabilities? Sen does not propose any singular formula as an answer. Rather, he proposes a general stance, an overall approach, a principled method, as indispensable for addressing these vital questions of social justice. What is involved is the discipline of reasoning, the pursuit of rationality, the submission of one's views to critical scrutiny, the requirement that one's judgement be informed by objectivity and impartiality. In the specification of these desiderata, Sen is in agreement with Rawls, though he differs, in numerous ways, on how to give content to these desiderata.

Rawls' criterion of social justice (encompassing the liberty and difference principles) is sought by Rawls to be justified as the unique social compact that will emerge from the bargaining of rational, self-interested agents acting behind the veil of ignorance in the original position. Sen, like others before him, questions the uniqueness of such an outcome. He also finds it limiting that 'justice as fairness' should emerge from the self-interest-oriented rationality underlying contractarian reasoning. The rationality assumed by much of mainstream economic theory, the version of it which informs 'rational choice theory', Sen finds even more seriously limiting as a guide to understanding the demands of justice. Rationality, within this framework, has generally been taken to be reflected uniquely in the objective of maximizing one's self-interest. Self-interest, in turn, is frequently interpreted so narrowly as to preclude a sense of well-being that arises from the contemplation of the well-being of *others*—what Adam Smith called 'sympathy'. Even if sympathy should be accommodated by a broader notion of self-interest than is conventionally allowed, there is no place here for 'commitment', which causes one to pursue (or desist from pursuing) a course of action not for reasons of self-interest but for ones of allegiance to some moral principle, say, or behavioural norm.

A view of rationality that would be more congenial to an appreciation of the demands of justice is one that assigns to reason the indispensable role of subjecting one's actions, views, and priorities to the test of *sustained critical scrutiny*. What matters for an appreciation of the requirements of fairness is not just one's own critical scrutiny, but the 'reasonable' critical scrutiny of others. Reason, in the end, cannot be restricted to what survives one's own examination without regard for others, but should go beyond, by allowing only such demands that we make as are immune to being reasonably rejected by *others*. Reasoning geared to the ends of justice, in short, must be informed by *objectivity* and *impartiality*.

Objectivity demands that the language employed in public reasoning should be shorn of prejudice, and of those idiosyncrasies and uniquely personal perspectives that constitute the bane of subjectivity: the presence of these elements in language could make the comprehension of its meaning difficult or impossible. Objectivity is, however, compatible with the particularity of the *position* from which one views phenomena, physical or ethical. Positional objectivity, for Sen, is not subjectivity. This is not to deny that positional objectivity might be compatible with illusion: the 'position' from which one views a phenomenon may be limited by 'poor vision'—by (depending upon the context of discussion) ignorance, illiteracy, the force of convention, 'false consciousness', and 'adaptive preferences'. Ethical reasoning must not be governed by these limitations: for an ethical precept to command conviction and credibility, it must be informed by a form of objectivity which accommodates the requirement of unbiasedness or *impartiality*.

Rawls' original position and the 'veil of ignorance' behind which the actors in the original position operate are intended to capture precisely this demand of impartiality. Sen questions whether the contractarian setting of the original position is either the only or the best way of capturing the dictates of impartiality. Indeed, for Sen, a superior model of impartiality is captured by Adam Smith's notion of the 'impartial spectator', one who brings to bear upon questions of justice a kind and degree of disinterestedness that may not be available to a contracting party engaged in a bargaining process, as in Rawls' original position. The Smithian impartial spectator affords the possibility of what Sen calls 'open impartiality', whereas the Rawlsian original position can accommodate only 'closed impartiality'. One consequence is that the original position excludes other countries from the ambit of consideration. Another is that it could fall prey to 'local parochialism'. Both these outcomes are inimical to the requirements of global justice, restricted, as they are, to considerations of intra-national justice. Apart from these 'exclusionary' limitations of the original position, the latter is also compatible with a certain 'inclusionary incoherence', revolving around the identification of the 'focal group' that is to be involved in the original position's deliberations: if the group in the original position is to decide on just institutions, and just institutions are to decide on the composition and size of the group constituting the just society, then the group in the original position need not be the one dictated by the decisions of just institutions. Open impartiality, for Sen, is a crucial ingredient of the reasoning that must inform one's idea of justice: it is an invitation to lift the limitations of 'poor vision' that can constrain positional objectivity, so that one is enabled to see, above all, that we owe goodwill and attentiveness to others as to ourselves, to those who may not be our immediate neighbours but are nevertheless part of the common world that we all inhabit.

Democracy and Human Rights

The highest expression of public reasoning is to be found in the institution we call democracy. Democracy is therefore an intimate part of Sen's idea of justice. It is often believed that democracy is a recent invention patented by the Western world, and Sen's historical discussion of alternative traditions of democracy and public reasoning in different parts of the world is a salutary corrective to this insular (and often enough arrogant) belief. Sen notes the significance, in contemporary discourses on justice, that has been accorded to democracy by two important philosophers—Rawls (1971) and Habermas (1995). For Sen, democracy in the cause of a just society must go beyond the *niti* (procedural) aspects of ballots and elections to embrace such desiderata as freedom of expression, the right to information, and the practice of public discussion. The importance, in this context, of a free media and of parliamentary democracy for the pursuit of justice is paramount. The absence of both weighed heavily in precipitating the tragedy of the Bengal Famine of 1943, when India was still under undemocratic colonial governance. It is, indeed, a remarkable statistic held out by Sen that no major famine has ever occurred in a functioning democracy. Casual empiricism has often been at the basis of the belief that development is best secured by rejecting the affectation of democratic governance (the examples of Singapore, South Korea, Hong Kong and Taiwan are frequently held out in support of the thesis): Sen not only finds little empirical support for this theory but also much support for the opposite view, that democracy aids rather than hinders development. The mechanical (and limited) identification of democracy with ballot procedures is often insensitive to the excesses of majoritarian rule vis-à-vis minority rights, and Sen explores the need, in the context of religion, for a more substantively fleshed-out notion of democracy than is entailed by a perfunctory concern for elections and voting.

Democracy is particularly important for securing one crucial requirement of a just society—the fulfilment of basic human rights. Sen presents a characteristically lucid discussion of the source, meaning, and justification of human rights. These rights are most profitably seen as claims on certain liberties (such as the liberty not to be subjected to baseless incarceration) and on certain freedoms (such as the ability to be well-nourished), which entail corresponding duties of delivery on the part of identified agents (the state, society, parents, particular persons, and so on). The *special* insistence on justification, which is often a feature of reactions to the discourse on human rights, is one which Sen finds puzzling: as he sees it, the existence of human rights is a matter that calls for no more justification than, say, the utilitarian claim that utility is important. But it is also a matter which calls for no *less* justification; and in either case, justification entails the use of reasoning and the exercise of critical scrutiny. One source of confusion on the logical and moral status of human rights has resided in Jeremy Bentham's insistence that human rights have no independent meaning if they have not already been enshrined in the law as justiciable claims. Sen notes that far from requiring human rights to be begotten by law, one should be able to see the desirability of law being begotten by a prior acknowledgement of the existence and moral standing of human rights. Legal means, however, are not the only ones available for the propagation of human rights: public reasoning, critical scrutiny, and advocacy are other instruments for this end. Sen conducts a particularly useful discussion on the plausibility of a collection of human rights encoded as 'social and economic rights'—the so-called 'second generation rights'. Objections to such rights have been based on the views that (a) they must be *institutionalized* (that is, there must be a clear specification of correlative duties and agents identified as the bearers of these duties) for these rights to be recognized as rights; and (b) they must be *feasible* of being sustained. Sen responds to both objections in a similar spirit, by proposing (a) that rather than deny a rights-status to an un-institutionalized claim, asserting its rights status may well be the right move towards institutionalizing it; and (b) that an unrealized right, rather than being dismissed as an infeasible ambition, should serve as an occasion for signalling 'a call for social action' in the cause of making it a realizable right.

Prelude to Some Critical Observations

So much for an attempt at a connected treatment of what I see as Sen's principal concerns in the book. I hope that I will at least escape the charge of having broken my promise of barbarism: however bluntly, I *have* endeavoured to summarize Sen's views on a number of the constitutive elements of his idea of justice—by covering the ground of capabilities, freedom, liberty, equality, rationality, objectivity, impartiality, global fairness, public reasoning, democracy, and human rights. Clearly, and whatever the shortfalls of my summary, it must be obvious to the reader that the idea of justice is a many-splendoured thing for Sen. Who can deny the breadth and depth and usefulness of these meditations—or the critical acumen, the original insights, and the magisterial scholarship underlying them? Having said this, however, one can yet entertain reservations with regard to certain aspects of the book. It is to some of these critical considerations that I now turn.

My reservations, really, boil down to a single reservation—namely that the book is much too Rawls-saturated. There is in the treatise a suggestion of excess both in the admiration of, and the points of departure from, Rawls. One can see this in the title itself: *The Idea of Justice* is, it seems, both an imitative tribute to *The Theory of Justice and* a firm statement of difference which asserts that what a student of justice ought to be after is not so much a theory of it, as an exploration of some of the ingredients that go into the making of its idea. The twin tendencies towards both celebration and criticism of Rawls are distracting and confusing: they make one wonder how such an allegedly brilliant philosopher could have got so many things so less than right. A briefer and more self-contained account of the debts to and contrasts from Rawls might have worked better.

Sometimes differences tend to be involuntarily sharpened in the keenness of controversy. Sen himself points out, on page 413—just two pages prior to the ending of the principal text: 'As this book is completed, I realize that I too have largely succumbed to the analytical temptation to concentrate on distinctions and to highlight contrasts.' Whether it is a matter of how the book has been written or how it has been read, it remains true that one reviewer has gone so far as to suggest that '…Sen sinks a knife into the heart of … [Rawls'] utopian program' (Romano 2009). In any event, there might be some independent merit to stressing the importance of not overdrawing certain distinctions between Sen's views on justice and those of Rawls and other Rawlsians. It is in this spirit that much of the discussion in what follows is carried out.

On the Institutions/Realizations and Resources/Capabilities Contrasts

First, in the useful distinction between the *nyaya* and *niti* conceptions of justice, there is no doubt that Sen leans on the side of *nyaya* and Rawls on the side of *niti*. But just as Sen is very far from dismissing the role of institutions in justice—how *could* anyone who has had any even passing thoughts on the institutions of the executive, the legislative and the judicial wings of government, or on the role of the press, or on free and fair elections? —so is Rawls very far from dismissing the 'social realizational' perspective of justice. This should be plain from the fact that the difference principle is essentially an 'end-state' principle of distributive justice, and speaks of social realization in the space (admittedly not of capabilities but) of an index of primary goods. Sen speaks of the desirability of a process-sensitive consequentialism, but equally Rawls may be construed as advancing the merits of an outcome-sensitive deontological perspective (although it may well be true that the purely 'procedural' view of justice has prevailed in much larger measure with certain other philosophers, such as Robert Nozick (1974)). Indeed, even in everyday thinking, most of us are persuaded of the importance of *both* institutional processes and social realizations for an overall assessment of the justness of a society. This is reflected, for instance, in the common (though no doubt simplified) perception that there are some societies like India with relatively just institutions (parliamentary democracy, a free press) in which people's lives go relatively poorly (low life expectancy and high illiteracy rates) and other societies like China with relatively unjust institutions (single-party, authoritarian government) in which people's lives go relatively well (low mortality and high literacy rates): Sen himself has done much, over his career, to highlight these issues. Sensitivity to both the institutions surrounding people and how their lives go cannot but be basic to an understanding of the requirements of a just society.

On the contrast between capabilities and resources, as I have pointed out earlier, Sen has made vitally important analytical contributions to an understanding of both inequality and poverty. An important issue to consider here is Sen's emphasis on the various alternative ways in which people can differ in their ability to convert resources into functionings. Without wishing (or necessarily being able) to legislate on the issue, I would draw the interested reader's attention to work by Thomas Pogge (2002a) in which he asserts that for all but *purely personal heterogeneities* (that is, capability differences among individuals which cannot in any way be traced to the working of social institutions at large), a 'sophisticated resourcist' of Rawlsian persuasion should indeed be able to take on board Sen's criticisms. (Where it comes to purely personal heterogeneities, there would appear to be a genuine cleavage, as between capabilists and resourcists, on the question of compensation for such interpersonal differences.) Importantly also, it would appear that the eventual *redress* of both inequality and poverty can only be effected with resources. It is resources that one redistributes or transfers: capabilities are not tangible things that one can take from person *A* to give to person *B*. Even in the matter of public goods, a state's ability to cater directly to its citizens' capabilities, such as in the matter of providing for drinking water or school education, is ultimately based on its ability to mobilize resources: the concern with GNP and its growth is not wholly benighted. It is possible to exaggerate the capabilities vs. resources contrast.

On Alternative Views of Impartiality

Thirdly, Rawlsian 'original position' impartiality comes out rather badly in Sen's comparison of it with the Smithian construct of the 'impartial spectator'. In defense of Rawls, I would first point out that there is something human-size about Rawls' appeal to individual rationality (as deference to self-interest) within a contractarian setting. The veil of ignorance confers upon the deliberators in the original position the attribute of impartiality-as-disinterestedness, but 'interestedness' is also so native and ungodlike a feature of humans that it appears to be both realistic and humble to appeal to that fact in arriving at a conception of justice. There is a further moral compulsion in seeing justice as fairness in the light of its being a product of a social compact: one can appeal to honour, to the sacredness of the word given, in enjoining on every agent the ethical imperative of being bound by the collective agreement to which she/he has voluntarily submitted. As Robert Bolt (1990) says in the preface to his play of Sir Thomas More, 'There is a special kind of shrug for a perjurer.' This must have some particular significance for a thinker like Rawls (1971) who held that 'justice is the first virtue of social institutions, as truth is of systems of thought'. Additionally, I must also admit to finding it hard to get a grip on what kind of *content* to give to the notion of the impartial spectator or to the notion of what cannot be reasonably rejected— except to imagine, unhelpfully, that an impartial spectator is one who spectates impartially, and that what cannot be reasonably rejected is what survives reasonable rejection. A charitable view of Rawls' original position would suggest that it is a flawed, but nevertheless ingenious, way of avoiding such question-begging.

Fourth, that the contractarian setting of Rawls' original position must necessarily entail some species of 'closed' impartiality, if not outright 'local parochialism', with adverse consequences for any viable theory of international as opposed to intra-national justice, is also not immediately apparent to me. I believe it is absolutely correct to point out that Rawls' *Law of Peoples* moves radically away from the spirit of *A Theory of Justice* (as we have noted earlier). Thomas Pogge (2004) has come down very heavily on the logical shortfalls of the *Law of Peoples*, its unexplained departures from the schema of *A Theory of Justice,* and the really rather disappointingly conservative view of international (as opposed to any truly global) justice that it advances. One of Pogge's principal complaints is that Rawls replaces the *persons* in his initial original position with *peoples* in the later original position. These clumsy manoeuvres, and the attendant violence they have done to the underlying spirit of normative individualism in Rawls' early work, appear to be the price Rawls has paid for the belief that global justice without some form of World Government is not possible. This also appears to be the view of Thomas Nagel (2005), and Sen cites his work in order to suggest that the framework of Rawls' original position in *A Theory of Justice* is simply not a viable one for any meaningful consideration of the notion of global justice. This view, however, is not compatible with that of a committed Rawlsian like Thomas Pogge whose 'cosmopolitan' view of global justice has been sought to be based, precisely, on an extension of the justice-as-fairness original position analysis to the global setting: the focal group here is constituted by the entire world's inhabitants, with the concern continuing to be with persons rather than with peoples. It is noteworthy that the cosmopolitanism of philosophers such as Pogge and Charles Beitz (1999) does not entail any sort of World Government, though it does entail the existence of supranational institutions engaged in governance (on which see Catherine Lu 2006). But such institutions already exist—the UN, the Bretton Woods twins, the European Union, WTO, to give a few examples—and the whole point of the quest for global justice by scholars in the Pogge and Beitz mould is to seek to replace the extremely unjust extant global institutional order with a just (or 'juster') one. To deny the potential for Rawlsian reasoning to yield any useful insights into the problem of global justice would appear to call for some substantial

neglect of the extraordinarily deep, principled, and varied work—
both empirical and theoretical—on global justice done by analysts
such as Thomas Pogge (2002b, 2002c, 2004, 2008). (The neglect
is justifiable, of course, if one subscribes to the view that Pogge is
mistaken in the belief that he is a Rawlsian!)

'Ideal Theory' in Rawlsian Justice

Fifth, Sen has a major quarrel with the entire approach to justice
comprehended in what he calls 'transcendental institutionalism'.
The latter is a specific instance of the deployment of what philosophers call 'ideal theory'. The problem of acceptability posed
by ideal theory is lucidly discussed in a paper by Laura Valentini
(2009). She points out that theories can be 'ideal' in two ways. As
applied to theories of justice, these latter could be ideal in the sense
(a) of employing idealized (false) assumptions, and (b) of prescribing a fully and perfectly rounded conceptualization of a just world
to which we should all aspire. Sen has difficulties with Rawlsian
transcendental institutionalism in both of these senses.

His critique of the first sense in which a theory can be ideal
is directed principally against the motivational aspects of human
behaviour underlying the Rawlsian focus on the 'background
structure' of just institutions. On page 8, he says: 'There is, obviously, a radical contrast between an arrangement-focused conception of justice and a realization-focused understanding: the latter
must, for example, concentrate on the actual behaviour of people, rather than presuming compliance by all with ideal behaviour.' One wonders if Rawls can be more productively seen as
presenting something like the Requirements of a Just Order, these
comprising: (a) the 'right' institutions; and (b) the 'right' individual behaviour. Ideal institutions and ideal personal behaviour are
then not so much assumptions about actual phenomena as descrip-
tive statements of conditions required for realizing a just order.
Again, on Page xi, Sen says of the Rawlsian approach: '...there
are some crucial inadequacies in this overpowering concentration
on institutions (where behaviour is assumed to be appropriately

compliant)....' But again, one wonders: 'assumed' or 'required'? Laws are written into a constitution on the presumption, or in the expectation, or within a contextual framework which postulates, that the officers of the court will implement the provisions of the law fairly and impartially, and will not, to the contrary, display corrupt and venal behaviour. One cannot blame the constitution, nor the enterprise of writing a constitution, for behavioural failure of the agents either entrusted with implementing, or bound by, the laws of the constitution. It is also not clear what else or more a constitution is expected to do, unless it be to devise 'incentive-compatible' mechanisms—mechanisms designed for institutions to cope with strategic behaviour by agents (which is a matter that Rawls himself does consider). Laura Valentini, in the work cited earlier, suggests that there is nothing intrinsically wrong with ideal theory, though it can be employed well or badly. A 'bad' example of ideal theory, for Valentini, is Rawls' law of peoples, while a 'good' example is justice as fairness. Responding to criticisms directed against the denial of discriminatory behaviour by agents in the Rawlsian (justice as fairness) schema, she notes that '...those facts about discrimination which are denied at the stage of theory construction can be taken into account at the level of application. In other words, Rawls' '... principles of domestic justice do not assume but prescribe the absence of such forms of discrimination' Valentini (2009). She goes on to say:

> Similar considerations can be advanced in relation to other Rawlsian and Dworkinian idealizations, such as perfect rationality, mutual disinterestedness, ignorance about one's self and preference authenticity. Since they are introduced at the level of the original position and 'desert island' thought experiments, such assumptions are part of the theories' overall 'devices of representation' (as Rawls would say) which are not meant to model existing human conditions. What these thought experiments articulate are the circumstances *under which* it seems plausible to construct a theory of justice, not the subjects or agents *to which* a theory of justice should apply. Rawls's and Dworkin's idealizations would indeed prevent their theories from being meaningfully action-guiding if they were somehow entailed by their principles, but they are not. In other words, the theories would fail to be action guiding *due* to their idealizations *if* fulfilling

their principles required citizens to be fully rational, their preferences to be independent and unbiased by prejudice and so forth. But this is not the case: such idealizations are not part of Rawls's and Dworkin's principles, they are merely part of the arguments supporting them. (Valentini 2009)

Comparative and Superlative Approaches to Justice

Sen is also, as we have noted, opposed to that aspect of 'transcendental institutionalism' which reflects ideal theory in the sense of prescribing a fully and perfectly rounded conceptualization of a just world to which we should all aspire. The difficulties which Sen perceives appear to have a number of sources. In discussing the 'comparative approach' which he favours, he suggests (page x) that 'The assumption that this comparative exercise cannot be undertaken without identifying, first, the demands of perfect justice, can be shown to be entirely incorrect...'. But it is not clear that the 'transcendental' approach either explicitly makes or entails this claim. Again, in his example involving the comparison of two paintings, Sen makes the point that da Vinci being the best is neither necessary nor sufficient for saying that Picasso is better than Dali. This is certainly true, but once more it is not clear that postulating da Vinci as the best somehow *prevents* one from comparing Picasso and Dali, which is surely not the case.

It may also be the case that in certain contexts the availability of a perfect theory has some advantages which the comparative approach lacks. Consider an example drawn from the literature on poverty measurement, and revolving around the justice-related activity of alleviating deprivation. Suppose we measure poverty (income poverty, to be specific) by the Foster–Greer–Thorbecke (1984) poverty measure P_2. (It does not really matter, for purposes of following the argument, if the reader should be unfamiliar with the content and properties of this poverty measure.) Given a certain distribution of income, imagine we have a budget of finite size S (not large enough to raise all the poor to the poverty line) available for allocation in order to alleviate poverty. Now consider a few alternative allocation strategies. Suppose x is a distribution in which all of S is allocated to the non-poor; y is a distribution in which, starting with the richest among the poor the income-gaps of the poor are bridged till the budget S is exhausted; w is a distribution in which the budget S is equally distributed among the poor; and u is a distribution in which S is allocated among the poor in proportion to their contribution to the aggregate poverty gap. Suppose every possible allocation of S is feasible. (There are infinitely many feasible allocations.) By computing the value of P_2 for each distribution, under the comparative approach it is certainly possible to recognize that, to the extent that a more poverty-reducing distribution is a more just distribution, y is more just than x, that w is more just than y and that u is more just than w. However, it can also be analytically established that the most just allocation of S, that is, the allocation which minimizes P_2, is one in which, starting from the poorest of the poor one exhausts the budget S through a sequence of income-equalizing transfers. This is the so-called 'lexicographic maximin solution'—a 'lexical' extension of Rawls' difference principle. One supposes it is meaningful to identify this solution and to implement it, rather than to content oneself with comparisons of distributions in arbitrarily specified sets. Thus, while there are contexts in which the comparative approach may be more productive than the transcendental one, there are also contexts in which things are the other way around.

Singular versus Plural Criteria of Justice

A major source of Sen's dissatisfaction with the transcendental approach resides in the presumption (as he puts it on Page 10) that '…there is basically only one kind of impartial argument, satisfying the demands of fairness … This, I would argue, may be a mistake.' It is instructive, in this context, to consider Sen's story of three children and a flute. Child A is the only one that knows how to play the flute; Child B is the most deprived of the three children, and Child C is the one that made the flute, unassisted. To whom should the flute be handed over? A Marxian criterion of justice, revolving around entitlement to the fruit of one's own labour, might advocate giving the flute to C; a Benthamite might prescribe giving the flute to A, from the consideration that, as the only one who knows how to make music from the flute she may occasion the greatest sum total of human happiness by having the flute in her possession; and the Rawlsian difference principle may require giving the flute to B. Each of these prescriptions engages our attention, each has something to commend it, and it is not clear that only any one of them may have a claim on our endorsement. Plurality, Sen seems to suggest, tends to defeat the transcendentalist insistence on a unique and perfect solution. It is useful, however, to remind oneself that a plurality of criteria of perfect justice is a product of several individual quests for singularity. In a world in which theorists of justice played safe by refusing to advance a notion of perfect justice, we should probably be the poorer for failing to see—in the context of Sen's example—that there are justice-related reasons for handing over the flute to *each* of A, B, and C (unless, of course, it is being suggested that each of us should have the imaginative capacity to visualize, all at once, the plural richness of Benthamite, Marxian, and Rawlsian approaches to the problem, thereby rendering the historical existence of Bentham, Marx, and Rawls largely irrelevant). In the end, *A Theory of Justice* is, after all, only *a* theory: this way of seeing it, I believe, enhances its utility; and it is this which I would take to be the moral of Sen's story.

Finally, on page 15, Sen says: 'If a theory is to guide reasoned choice of policies, strategies, or institutions, then the identification of fully just social arrangements is neither necessary nor sufficient.' This is true. It is also true, though, that such an identification *is* necessary under a more demanding ambition—one that requires of a theory of justice that it be a guide to the reasoned choice of *the most just* policies, strategies and institutions. This sentiment is more than a tautology: it expresses the view that choices about what a theory of justice should aim at are not informed only by considerations of economy and sufficiency dictated by clear-sightedness and analytical unclutteredness, but also by notions of what special obligations a philosopher feels she/he ought to labour under. In this view, the goal a philosopher sets for oneself is a declaration of one's philosophical predilections rather than an end determined exclusively, or even largely, by the demands of analytical prudence. In other words, there is an element of personal psychology here that might warrant attention: the possibility that there could be, within a philosopher's mind, a link between the arduousness and riskiness of the task one has set for oneself and the authenticity of one's philosophical pursuits. In Rawls' transcendentalist approach, there is something of both the vulnerability and grandeur of Camus' Sisyphus. In the end, that approach may simply be saying something about Rawls himself, because a philosopher's philosophy often carries upon itself a certain stamp of the autobiographical. As Nietzsche (1968 [1885]: 203) wrote: 'Gradually it has become clear to me what every great philosophy so far has been: namely, the personal confession of its author and a kind of involuntary and unconscious memoir....'

A Summing-up

At the end of this long journey, I learn the wisdom of walking on both legs. In seeking to apprehend the contours of justice through reasoning, it is helpful to be seized of the importance of social realizations *and* transcendental institutionalism; the comparative *and* the superlative; outcomes *and* processes; consequentialism *and* deontology; and capabilities *and* resources. The famous 1960s Stanley Kramer film *Inherit The Wind* (about the defense of a young schoolmaster on trial for teaching evolution in a small Southern US school) ends with the Clarence Darrow lawyer-figure, played by Spencer Tracey, walking out of the courtroom with a copy of the Holy Bible under one arm and a copy of Darwin's *Origin of Species* under the other. Corny and sentimental, one might say. And yet, I believe a student of justice can do worse than walk out of a library with a copy of *A Theory* under one arm and a copy of *The Idea* under the other.

References

Arrow, K.J. (1963), *Social Choice and Individual Values* (Second Edition). New York: Wiley.

Beitz, C. (1999), 'International Liberalism and Distributive Justice: A Survey of Recent Thought', *World Politics*, 51(2): 269–96.

Bolt, R. (1990), *A Man For All Seasons: A Play in Two Acts*. New York: A Vintage Book.

Foster, J., J. Greer, and E. Thorbecke (1984), 'A Class of Decomposable Poverty Measures', *Econometrica*, 52(3): 761–6.

Habermas, J. (1995), 'Reconciliation through the Public Use of Reason: Remarks on John Rawls's *Political Liberalism*', *Journal of Philosophy*, 92(3): 109–31.

Lu, C. (2006), 'World Government', in Edward N. Zalta (ed.), *The Stanford Encyclopedia of Philosophy*. Stanford University: The Metaphysics Research Lab.

Nagel, T. (2005), 'The Problem of Global Justice', *Philosophy and Public Affairs*, 33(2): 113–47.

Nietzsche, F.W. (1968 [1885]), 'Beyond Good and Evil', in W. Kaufmann (trans. and ed.), *Basic Writings of Nietzsche*. New York: The Modern Library, p. 203.

Nozick, R. (1974), *Anarchy, State, and Utopia*. New York: Basic Books.

Nussbaum, M.C. (2000), *Women and Human Development: The Capabilities Approach*. Cambridge: Cambridge University Press.

Pogge, T.W. (2002a), 'Can the Capability Approach be Justified?', in M. Nussbaum and C. Flanders (eds), *Global Inequalities*, in *Philosophical Topics* (special issue), 30(2): 167–228.

———. (2002b), 'Moral Universalism and Global Economic Justice', *Politics, Philosophy and Economics*, 1(1): 29–58.

———. (2002c), *World Poverty and Human Rights: Cosmopolitan Responsibilities and Reforms*. Cambridge: Polity Press.

———. (2004), 'The Incoherence Between Rawls's Theories of Justice', *Fordham Law Review*, 72(5): 101–21.

———. (2008), 'What is Global Justice?', *Revista de Economia Institucional*, 10(19): 99–114 (English trans.).

Rawls, J. (1971), *A Theory of Justice*. Cambridge, MA: Harvard University Press.

———. (1999), *The Law of Peoples: With 'The Idea of Public Reason Revisited'*. Cambridge, MA: Harvard University Press.

Romano, C. (2009), 'Amartya Sen Shakes Up Justice Theory', *Chronicle of Higher Education*, 14 September. Available at: http://chronicle.com/article/Amartya-Sen-Shakes-Up-Justice/48332.

Sen, A. (1970), 'The Impossibility of a Paretian Liberal', *Journal of Political Economy*, 78(1): 152–7.

———. (1973), *On Economic Inequality*. Oxford: Clarendon Press.

———. (1980), 'Equality of What?', in S.M. McMurrin (ed.), *Tanner Lectures on Human Values, I*. Salt Lake City/Cambridge: University of Utah Press/Cambridge University Press.

———. (1983), 'Poor, Relatively Speaking', *Oxford Economic Papers*, 35(2): 153–69.

Valentini, L. (2009), 'On the Apparent Paradox of Ideal Theory', *mimeo*, Political Science, University College London.

12

Are Egalitarians Really Vulnerable to the Levelling-down Objection and the Divided World Example?*

Motivation

Derek Parfit's (1997) essay on priority and equality suggests that egalitarianism is vulnerable to what he calls the Levelling-Down Objection and the Divided World Example. This is a source of potential concern for economists and philosophers who regard themselves in the light of egalitarians. How much of an actual concern to egalitarians should Parfit's criticism be? The present note is an attempt by an economist to respond to this query.

It should be clarified that there is no specific 'economist's case', as such, that is pushed in this note. Rather, the question is one of putting to work a general approach of 'formalism' and 'precision' which has come to be associated with mainstream economics in the cause of clarifying a philosophical problem. More specifically, and with reference to the present context, it appears that Parfit's critique of egalitarianism can be meaningfully addressed by taking

*This article was originally published, under the same title, in *Journal of Philosophical Economics*, IV(2): Spring 2011.

care to define the notion of 'Pluralist Telic Egalitarianism' in a reasonably clear, transparent and self-contained manner, as is sought to be done in this note. This does not entail the use of mathematics, leave alone the higher mathematics; but it does underline the utility of minimizing ambiguity in the use of language, and of stating one's claim more rather than less precisely, so as to promote the chances of the claim being challenged without being misunderstood.

This note is primarily substantive, not methodological, in orientation. Nevertheless, it may be useful to briefly complete the methodological point flagged in the preceding paragraph. Deirdre McCloskey (2002) has pointed to two besetting sins to which economics is prone: the sin of 'qualitative theorems' and the sin of 'statistical significance', which together are held to serve poorly the cause of thought and observation as means to an understanding of the world in which we live. Confining oneself to the first of these identified sins, it may be noted that a cardinal feature of 'qualitative theorems' is the emphasis on precision and formalism, such as is characteristic of the axiomatic method pursued in much of this tradition. It should not be hard to see that 'qualitative theorems' of the variety which economics abounds in, constitute a sin when they purport to be descriptions about the real world. But can, and do, 'qualitative theorems' serve other purposes than as (sadly deficient) descriptions or explanations of actual economic phenomena on the ground?

Many would suggest 'yes'. Frank Hahn's (1973) essay on Janos Kornai's critique of General Equilibrium Theory (GET) is a case in point. Hahn suggests that if it were not for the fundamental and formal results of Arrow-Debreu GET, it would be hard to undermine the wisdom of the 'folk theorem' underlying Adam Smith's Invisible Hand account of the economy: it is thanks to the precision and care of the Arrow-Debreu formulation of the problem that we are enabled, so easily, to see the essentially profoundly unreal conditions under which the basic theorems of welfare economics hold. Partha Dasgupta (2002) makes a similar point about the prolonged debate on Marx's account of how to solve the problem of determining the exchange value of a commodity, and invites Marxist scholars to provide an intelligible formalization of Marx that would advance the possibility of both understanding and debate.

The point can be made even more forcefully in the context of 'normative' reasoning and the tradition of internal criticism in economics. Consider the case of the apparently plausible 'compensation' criteria that were a prominent feature of the 'new' welfare economics of the 1930s and 1940s: it took a good deal of careful formal work to unravel the logical problems associated with these criteria. More generally, the entire programme of the 'new' welfare economics, with its emphasis on assessing the goodness of alternative states of the world solely on the basis of data on the ordinal and interpersonally non-comparable utilities of the individuals constituting a society, was effectively derailed by Kenneth Arrow's (1963) General Possibility Theorem—itself a product of a careful formalization of the (often vaguely verbal) claims and assumptions permeating the 'new' welfare economics.

So, if there is any 'methodological' point to the present essay, then it relates to the restricted claim that while a considerable quantity of 'mainstream' economics (arguably) employs mathematics or formalism in the cause of pretentious and hollow 'theorem-mongering', there are also constructive uses to which the tradition (or habit) of formalization can be put. One of these is to clarify the basis of claims made in positive and normative reasoning, and thereby to advance the possibility of disagreement founded in understanding rather than misunderstanding. This note is an effort at illustrating this point of view in the context of a philosophical problem concerning egalitarianism raised by Derek Parfit. The rest of the note will be devoted entirely to a substantive consideration of this problem.

The Problem

An aspect of Parfit's thesis can be summarized along the following lines. There are situations in which, though one may be disposed to judge an equitable distribution with a smaller sum of well-being to be superior to a less equitable distribution with a larger sum of well-being, there is really no egalitarian argument available to rationalize such a judgement. An egalitarian argument must be based on either (a) the view that an equal distribution of benefits is, in itself, good; or (b) the view that striving for equality, on grounds of justice or fairness (or some other value), is the right thing to do. Egalitarians of persuasion (a) are *Telic* Egalitarians, and those of persuasion (b) are *Deontic* Egalitarians.

The view that equality is, in itself, a good thing cannot plausibly be maintained in the face of the Levelling-Down Objection, which is the objection that there is no respect in which a change for greater equality achieved by simply dragging the better-off down to the level of the worse-off can be good. This leaves one with the Deontic Egalitarian argument to deal with. Here, however, one can conceive of situations in which a distribution may be unequal but the inequality cannot be attributed to any failure of justice or fairness, etc., nor are there any unfavourable effects following from the inequality. A situation with these features is encapsulated in an account of what Parfit calls the Divided World Example.

In this Example, one has (as it were), two Worlds—World 1 and World 2, which are hermetically sealed and insulated from each other (in the sense that neither world has any knowledge of the other's existence). Each world consists of n persons. Now consider three distributions: $p \equiv (100, 200)$, $q \equiv (145, 145)$, and $r \equiv (150, 150)$, where p is to be understood as representing a distribution in which each person in World 1 receives a benefit of 100 units of well-being and each person in World 2 receives a benefit of 200 units, and q and r are to be analogously interpreted. The problem presented by the Divided World Example is to rank the distributions p and q. Parfit suggests that it would be reasonable to pronounce q as being a better distribution than p, though there may be no egalitarian justification available for this preference. In particular, in the Divided World, Deontic Egalitarianism is of no avail in supporting a preference for the equal distribution with a smaller mean over the unequal distribution with a larger mean (on which see Parfit (1997, p. 205): 'since the two groups are unaware of each other's existence, this inequality was not deliberately produced or maintained. Since this inequality does not involve wrong-doing, there is no injustice.') Such a preference requires some view, other than an egalitarian one, to rationalize it. Parfit's rationalization is in terms of what he calls the Priority View.

In this note, the concern will not be with the merits of the Priority View, nor even with what the Priority View *is*, but only with the alleged vulnerability of egalitarianism to the Levelling-Down Objection and the Divided World Example, which necessitates the quest for some other (non-egalitarian) view, such as the Prioritarian View. In what follows, the question is first addressed of whether the force of the Levelling-Down Objection is as compelling as it may appear to be. Second, some reservations one could entertain about the reach of the Divided World Example are discussed. The line of reasoning pursued in this note shares similarities with that employed in Christiano and Braynen (2008).

On the Levelling-down Objection

Parfit claims that the Levelling-Down Objection is an embarrassment to those whom he calls Telic Egalitarians. A closer look at the issue, however, suggests that this claim is valid only for those whom he calls Pure Telic Egalitarians, and not for those whom he calls Pluralist Telic Egalitarians. Both kinds of Telic Egalitarian are seen as subscribing to the *Principle of Equality*, which is the principle that 'it is in itself bad if some people are worse off than others' (Parfit 1997, p. 204). The distinction between Pure and Pluralist Telic Egalitarians is spelt out in the following terms by Parfit (1997, p. 205):

> If we cared only about equality, we would be *Pure* Egalitarians. If we cared only about utility, we would be Utilitarians. Most of us accept a pluralist view: one that appeals to more than one principle or value. According to *Pluralist Egalitarians*, it would be better both if there was more equality, and if there was more utility. In deciding which of the two outcomes would be better, we give weight to both these values.

The above suggests that there are different ways in which one can give content to the view that 'it is in itself bad if some people are worse off than others'. These different ways then serve to provide a taxonomy of Telic Egalitarians. It is useful to try and state the distinctions involved as sharply as possible. It would also be fair to permit the distinctions to work in such a way that differentiation is achieved through a specification of what is minimally required in order to mark the relevant, and crucial, point of departure. With this in mind, the following characterizations of the Pure and the Pluralist Telic Egalitarian are offered. It seems reasonable to believe that these characterizations, although parsimoniously effected, are compatible with Parfit's descriptions. It is important to underline that there are no ready-made, 'officially sanctioned' definitions or characterizations available: what are here provided, one can claim, are adequate to their purpose and, in particular, one could assert that it would simply be coercive to *require* of a Pluralist Telic Egalitarian that she embrace any belief beyond what has been attributed to her in the ensuing description.

Pure Telic Egalitarianism requires that, given any two equi-dimensional distributions of well-being, the more equal distribution be judged to be the better one.

Pluralist Telic Egalitarianism requires that, given any two equi-dimensional distributions of well-being with the same sum total of well-being, the more equal distribution be judged to be the better one; and given any two equal equi-dimensional distributions of well-being, the distribution with the larger sum total of well-being be judged to be the better one. (In the interests of brevity, certain reasonable qualifications are here suppressed. One such *caveat*, for instance, would be that the preference for equality could be waived in a 'life-boat dilemma' sort of situation wherein the average level of well-being is less than what may be required to achieve 'survival', or some minimally acceptable human life.)

Let $\mathbf{v} = (10, 100)$ and $\mathbf{w} = (10, 10)$ be two 2-person distributions of well-being. $\mathbf{w}$ can be seen to have been derived from $\mathbf{v}$ through a 'levelling down' of one person's well-being. A Pure Telic Egalitarian is committed to judging that $\mathbf{w}$ is a better distribution than $\mathbf{v}$. The Pluralist Telic Egalitarian is, however, not committed to any such judgement, since $\mathbf{v}$ and $\mathbf{w}$ do not share the same sum total of well-being. For the same reason, the Pluralist Telic Egalitarian is not even committed to the judgement that $\mathbf{w}$ is a better distribution than $\mathbf{v}$ in *some* way: she is being asked to compare two distributions which do not meet the requirements under which she feels she can, given her beliefs, plausibly undertake a comparison. She can legitimately counter the charge that she is compromising her professed belief in the *intrinsic* value of equality by responding thus: 'It is perfectly consistent for me to maintain that inequality, in itself, is bad, *in the sense and to the extent*, that an equal distribution of a given sum total of well-being is better than an unequal distribution. I am in no way guilty of a violation of this claim if I refuse to pronounce that **w** is, in *some* way, a better distribution than **v**. I may add that the way in which the claim is addressed amounts to a non-trivial deference to the demands of equality—such as would not, for instance, be accommodated by a principle of the type of sufficientarianism'. One may respond to this by insisting that for a person to qualify for the description of 'Egalitarian', she would have to go beyond judgements on equity relating to fixed-sum distributions, and be prepared to endorse the view, in different-sum comparisons, that one distribution is better than the other in *one* respect, that of equality—thus, presumably, paving the way for the charge of discerning some virtue in Levelling Down. Such a response strikes this author as being somewhat perverse: it is a little like insisting that not swearing is a requirement of decency, the better, subsequently, to castigate a well-spoken person for his priggishness! There is an element of the Double Bind here, which is entirely avoidable. And once it is avoided, it becomes clear that the Levelling-Down Objection applies only to the Pure Telic Egalitarian. But this in itself spells no trouble for egalitarianism in general, nor even for Telic Egalitarianism in general. A Pure Telic Egalitarian is clearly some kind of fanatic, as one must expect a Pure Anything to be. One specific variety of egalitarian does not speak for all egalitarians. Arising from this, one is not obliged to see the Levelling-Down objection as constituting a particularly compelling problem for egalitarians (considered in their generality) to contend with.

Parfit, however, seems to believe that all of Telic Egalitarianism is disposed of by the Levelling-Down Objection. His line of reasoning, leading up to his Priority View, seems to be as follows:

(a)   Egalitarianism can be Telic or Deontic.
(b)   The Divided World Example does not afford the Deontic Egalitarian any equality-related argument for judging outcome **q** to be better than outcome **p**, though intuition (to

begin with), and subsequent consideration (entailing a conversion to the Priority View), may suggest that outcome **q** is to be preferred.

(c)   An egalitarian preference for outcome **q**, then, can be attributed only to Telic Egalitarianism, that is, to belief in the Principle of Equality which asserts that inequality, in itself, is bad.

(d)   But the Levelling-Down Objection is an objection to the Telic view.

(e)   Consequently, neither Telic nor Deontic Egalitarianism, whose union constitutes Egalitarianism, can deliver the judgement that outcome **q** is to be preferred to outcome **p**.

If (a)–(e) is a fair summary of Parfit's line of reasoning, then the flaw in it should be apparent: (d) is the weak link in the chain. Proposition (d) (the Levelling-Down Objection is an Objection to the Telic view) has not in fact been established by Parfit: he has demonstrated that the *Pure* Telic view could fall foul of the Levelling-Down Objection. This is not to assert that the Pluralist Telic view (such as has been presented here and sought to be justified) has anything to commend (or oppose) it, only that Parfit's case against it is not known.

On the Divided World Example

Further, one can question the view that the Divided World Example does not afford an egalitarian any equality-related argument for judging outcome **q** to be better than outcome **p**. Recalling that a Pluralist Telic Egalitarian is not necessarily undone by the Levelling-Down Objection, it is open to such an egalitarian to invoke distribution $\mathbf{r} \equiv (150, 150)$ which, in view of her belief that an equal distribution of a given sum of well-being is preferable to an unequal distribution, she will prefer to the distribution $\mathbf{p} = (100, 200)$. In view also of her belief that of two equal distributions of well-being, the one with the larger sum of well-being is preferable, she will prefer r = (150, 150) to q = (145, 145). It is, further, reasonable for this Pluralist Telic Egalitarian to suggest that she has a mild preference for r over q because the latter, in comparison with the former, reflects a relatively small sacrifice of total well-being at a given level of equality, and that she has a strong preference for r over p because the latter, in comparison with the former, reflects a relatively large sacrifice of equality at a given level of total well-being. Since the extent to which this egalitarian prefers r over p is greater than the extent to which she prefers r over q, she has a defensible egalitarian reason for preferring q over p—even in a World that is Divided.

Concluding Note

This note has been concerned to show that there is a non-trivial way in which the notion of Telic Egalitarianism can be defined such that it attends to the virtues of both size and distribution in comparisons of alternative regimes of well-being. Such a view of Telic Egalitarianism upholds the view that inequality, in itself, is bad, while subscribing also to the view that—other things equal—an outcome with more well-being is preferable to one with less well-being. A crucial feature of this perfectly defensible conception of egalitarianism is that it entails no commitment to the view that any equal distribution is preferable to any unequal distribution in at least one respect, that of equality. As such, the conception is proof against the strictures of the Levelling-Down Objection. Furthermore, and as has been shown in the note, the formulation of Telic Egalitarianism advanced here enables one to present an egalitarian justification for preferring an equal distribution of a smaller sum total of well-being to an unequal distribution of a larger sum total, even within the potentially problematic context of Parfit's Divided World setting. It seems fair to conclude that, all things considered, the Levelling-Down Objection and the Divided World Example are not, after all, fatal worries for the ethic of egalitarianism.

References

Arrow, K.J. (1963), *Social Choice and Individual Values*. New York: John Wiley & Sons, Inc.

Christiano, T. and W. Braynen (2008), 'Inequality, Injustice and Leveling Down', *Ratio*, 21(4): 392–420.

Dasgupta, P. (2002),'Modern Economics and its Critics', in U. Maki (ed.) *Fact and Fiction in Economics: Models, Realism and Social Construction*. Cambridge: Cambridge University Press.

Hahn, F. (1973), 'The Winter of Our Discontent', *Economica* (new series), 40(159): 322-30.

McCloskey, D. (2002), *The Secret Sins of Economics*. Prickly Paradigm Press: Chicago.

Parfit, D. (1997), 'Equality and Priority', *Ratio (new series)*, 10(3): 202–21.

13

Can We Possibly Subscribe to Both Liberty and Equality at One and the Same Time?*,+

The Problem

A 'good society' is one which is governed by a number of prized social virtues. Among these virtues, surely, must be counted a deference to the values of personal liberty and interpersonal equity. (These, after all, are two of the three values embodied in the French Revolution's stirring exhortation to 'Liberty, Equality, and Fraternity'!) In urging, or professing, an acceptance of these values, there is the implicit judgement that the acceptance entails no possible problem of internal coherence or logical consistency. In this small essay, it will be shown that the apparently unproblematic judgement just mentioned could prove to be suspect. In particular, the reader is invited to consider that there are plausible, but mutually incompatible, ways in which the principles of 'liberty' and 'equity'

* First published in *Think: Journal of the Royal Institute of Philosophy*, 11(30): 103–10, (2012).

+ This essay is a highly simplified and informal version of a somewhat technical paper of the present author's (Subramanian 2010). I would like to thank, without implicating, Jerry Kelly for helpful suggestions on an earlier draft of the article.

can be formulated. The essay draws on the conventions and methods of a body of knowledge called 'social choice theory', which lies at the intersection of philosophy, political science and economics.

Background: Social Choice Theory and 'Impossibility Theorems'

One of the commonest problems faced by any society is the following one: given the preference rankings of a group of individuals over a set of alternatives, how should these rankings be aggregated into a single ranking which may be taken to be a reasonable ranking of the alternatives for the society as a whole? How, that is, may a society arrive at a *social* ranking of alternatives from information on the *individual* rankings of these alternatives? One method, which we are all very familiar with, is the elementary majority decision rule, or, as it is sometimes called, the Method of Majority Decision (MMD). MMD simply requires that, in the pair-wise choice from any pair of alternatives x and y, if a majority of individuals prefer x to y, then x should be socially preferred to y. Simple though it is, MMD is vulnerable to a problem of internal consistency, one which is popularly known as the *Paradox of Voting*. Here is the paradox.

Imagine a society comprising three individuals, whom we shall call 1, 2 and 3, respectively. Suppose there are three alternatives—think of these as candidates in an election—named x, y and z, respectively. Suppose further, that individual preferences are described by the following: 1 prefers x to y and y to z; 2 prefers z to x and x to y; and 3 prefers y to z and z to x. Notice now that a majority of individuals (1 and 2) prefer x to y, and a majority (1 and 3) prefer y to z. MMD will dictate that x be socially preferred to y and y socially preferred to z. The logical property of *transitivity* will now demand that x be socially preferred to z. (Transitivity is a necessity of logic imposed on triples: for example, if we are talking of the relation 'taller than', and if it is given that Ashoo is taller than Babloo and Babloo is taller than Chutki, then transitivity will entail that Ashoo is taller than Chutki.) However, a majority of individuals (2 and 3) prefer z to x, so MMD will require z to be socially preferred to x. But, clearly, we cannot have both x socially preferred to z and z socially preferred to x at the same time—and it is this contradiction, precipitated by the MMD, which is encompassed in the Paradox of Voting.

'Social choice theory' is concerned with an examination of the logical problems of preference aggregation—the Paradox of Voting is an example—in a variety of settings. A number of distinguished names have been associated with the evolution of this branch of study—including Jean-Charles de Borda and Marquis de Condorcet in the 18 century; Charles Lutwidge Dodgson (somewhat better known as Lewis Carroll) in the 19 century; and Duncan Black, Kenneth Arrow, Michael Dummett and Amartya Sen, among others, in the 20th and 21st centuries. Arrow, in particular, proved a quite remarkable result, incongruously named 'The General Possibility Theorem' (which appeared in a book, published in 1963, called *Social Choice and Individual Values*). The result pointed to the logical impossibility of there being any rule of preference aggregation which could satisfy a small number of apparently very reasonable, undemanding, and innocuous principles of social choice.

Subsequently, Sen (in a brief paper titled 'The Impossibility of a Paretian Liberal' which appeared in a 1970 issue of the *Journal of Political Economy*) established that there is a specific and well-defined sense in which a widely employed criterion of 'efficiency' employed by economists, the so-called Pareto Principle, is incompatible with a very weak criterion of liberty which he called Minimal Liberalism. Social choice theory, for reasons of a great proliferation of demonstrations of this nature, has acquired a reputation for being the natural home of 'impossibility results'.

Sen was also the author of a simple and appealing principle of equality called the Weak Equity Axiom, which appears in a book of his called *On Economic Inequality* (1973). The axiom essentially demands that, in a distribution of income between two individuals, a larger share ought to go to the uniformly more disadvantaged person (such as in the division of an income of given size between an able-bodied and a physically challenged person, the assumption being that at every level of income, the latter individual is worse-off than the former). Peter Hammond is an economist who has offered an axiomatic justification of a certain celebrated criterion of justice due to the philosopher John Rawls. In the process, he provided a generalization of Sen's Weak Equity Axiom to social choice situations which go beyond pure income-distribution problems (Hammond's essay, 'Equity, Arrow's Conditions, and Rawls' Difference Principle', appeared in a 1976 issue of the journal *Econometrica*). In what follows, we shall employ Sen's principle of Minimal Liberalism and a version of Hammond's Weak Equity principle in order to analyse what might be called the Problem of the Possibility of Liberal Egalitarianism.

On Two Specific Types of Pairs of Alternatives

In formulating our principles of liberty and equity, we shall take the assistance of Alan Gibbard ('A Pareto Consistent Libertarian Claim', published in 1974 in the *Journal of Economic Theory*). But first, *alternatives*, or *social states*, will, as is customary, be taken to be complete descriptions of society including each person's state of being and doing in it. Typically, social states will be designated x, y, z, etc. *Individuals* will be designated 1, 2, 3, ... , i, ... , n.

A pair of states x and y will be termed *i-variants* if they differ only with respect to a feature which may be deemed to be personal to individual i. Thus, if x and y differ from each other only in the respect that in x person 1 is whistling a tune in his bathroom and in y he is not doing so, then x and y are a pair of 1-variants; if w and z differ only in the respect that in w person 3 is drinking grape juice and in z she is drinking orange juice, then w and z are a pair of 3-variants and so on.

Similarly, a pair of states x and y will be termed *j,k-variants* if they differ only with respect to features which may be deemed to be personal to individuals j and k. Thus, if s is a state in which person 2 is singing in his bathroom and person 4 is drinking grape juice, while t is a state which is identical to s in all respects save that in t, person 2 is silent in his bathroom and person 4 is drinking orange juice, then s and t are a pair of 2,4-variants.

Minimal Liberty

Now it seems reasonable to demand, in a libertarian world, that if x and y are a pair of i-variants, then i's preference over the states x and y ought to count as the social preference over that pair: after all, the two states differ only in a matter of personal relevance to i, so i's personal preference ranking of the states ought to be socially decisive. It may be construed as being minimally liberal to allow at least two individuals such social decisiveness over a pair of alternatives each. *Minimal liberty*, therefore, can be taken to demand the following: there should be at least two individuals j and k and two pairs of alternatives $\{x,y\}$ and $\{w,z\}$, with x and y being a pair of j-variants and w and z being a pair of k-variants, such that if j prefers x to y (respectively, y to x), then society should prefer x to y (respectively, y to x), and if k prefers w to z (respectively, z to w), then society should prefer w to z (respectively, z to w).

Weak Equity

Suppose x and y to be a pair of j,k-variants. Since x and y differ only with respect to features which are personal to j and k, it can be argued that it is only the preferences of j and k over the alternatives x and y which ought to matter for the social ranking of x and y. How might an equity-conscious ethic determine the manner in which j's and k's preference rankings of x and y should influence the social ranking of x and y? Consider the following plausible generalization of the spirit underlying Sen's Weak Equity Axiom. Suppose j is uniformly more advantaged than k, in the specific sense that everybody in society would rather be person j than person k in the state x, and would similarly rather be person j than person k in the state y. That is to say, suppose that no matter in which state, it is unanimously held to be better to be j than to be k. Then, it seems to be compatible with the requirements of equity to demand that it is the uniformly more disadvantaged individual k's preference ranking over the pair of states $\{x,y\}$ which should determine the social ranking of the pair. This (with some modifications) captures Hammond's formulation of a generalization of Sen's axiom. *Weak Equity*, therefore, may be taken to demand the following: for any pair of j,k-variants x and y, if j is considered by everybody in society to be better off than k in each of the states x and y, and if j prefers x to y while k prefers y to x, then y should be socially preferred to x (in 'equity-sensitive' partisanship with the relatively disadvantaged individual k).

Liberty, Equity, and Impossibility

It can be shown that in a situation which does not proscribe any logically possible pattern of individual preferences, and in which the social ranking of alternatives is required to be transitive, the principles of minimal liberty and weak equity, as we have defined them, are mutually incompatible. A precise statement of the relevant results, with proofs, is available in a recent paper by this author (Subramanian 2010). For the present, the following example, which takes some liberties with a Wodehousean situation, should suffice to highlight the essential nature of the underlying difficulty.

Police Constable Oates would give anything to ensure that the dog Bartholomew does not accompany his mistress Stephanie Byng on her walks, for there is between man and dog a deep-seated enmity. If Bartholomew makes unfriendly noises at Oates, it is, in Miss Byng's view, because Oates is aggravating the dog by doing his beat on a bicycle when the right thing to do would be for him to walk which, according to Miss Byng (although Oates does not regard this as being the 'point at tissue'), would also help in knocking off some of the policeman's fat.

We can now define the following social states. x is a state in which Miss Byng is accompanied on her walks by her dog, and Oates does his beat on a bicycle; y is identical to x in all respects save that in y Oates does his beat on foot; and z is identical to y in all respects save that in z Miss Byng leaves her dog behind at home.

Clearly, the states x and y, being a pair of 'Oates-variants', are in Oates' 'protected sphere', while similarly, the states y and z, being a pair of 'Miss-Byng variants', are in Miss Byng's 'protected sphere'. Since other things equal the policeman prefers travelling by bicycle to travelling on foot, and Miss Byng prefers travelling with Bartholomew to travelling without him, the principle of minimal liberty assures us that x is socially preferred to y and y is socially preferred to z whence, by transitivity, x should be socially preferred to z.

Assume further (a) that Miss Byng prefers state x to state z (her overriding concern is that the dog Bartholomew should accompany her on her walks); (b) that Oates prefers state z to state x (never mind if he has to do his beat on foot, so long as he does not have to have his day blighted by an encounter with that dog); and (c) that in any neutral ethical observer's eye, Oates' welfare level (possibly by virtue of his being a policeman which, according to Wodehouse, makes for a generally jaundiced view of life) is lower than Miss Byng's in both states x and z. Given this, and noting that the pair of states $\{x,z\}$ is a pair of 'Byng, Oates-variants', the principle of Weak Equity will dictate that z is socially preferred to x. But this contradicts 'x socially preferred to z', derived earlier. In the improbable contingency that Sir Watkyn Basset, Justice of the Peace for Totleigh-on-the-Wold, cared to serve the interests of both equity and individual liberty, he should find himself in a tight spot.

Concluding Observations

I conclude by desisting from addressing queries—which I leave to the reader (if she/he is still there) to ponder—such as (a) what is the source of the contradiction established in this paper? (b) what are some possible 'escape routes' from the liberty–equity dilemma? and (c) what significance might the impossibility result have for our notions of liberty and equality?

References

Arrow, Kenneth J. (1963), *Social Choice and Individual Values* (Second Edition). New York: John Wiley and Sons.

Gibbard, Alan (1974), 'A Pareto Consistent Libertarian Claim', *Journal of Economic Theory*, 7(4): 388–410.

Hammond, Peter J. (1976), 'Equity, Arrow's Conditions, and Rawls' Difference Principle', *Econometrica*, 44(4): 793–804.

Sen, Amartya K. (1970), 'The Impossibility of a Paretian Liberal', *Journal of Political Economy*, 78(1): 152–9.

———. (1973), *On Economic Inequality*. Clarendon: Oxford University Press.

Subramanian, S. (2010), 'Liberty, Equality, and Impossibility: Some General Results in the Space of "Soft" Preferences', *Journal of Economic Policy Reform*, 13(4): 325–41.

PART III

Miscellaneous Mistakes

14

A Curmudgeon's Complaints*

'Bah!' said Scrooge; 'humbug!'

Indian Cricket

One does not have to be a curmudgeon to recognize that there is much that is wrong with Indian cricket, though being a curmudgeon (both with specific reference to the present context and as a general virtue) certainly does not hinder the cause. Indian cricket is a subject that attracts gripes not only against itself but also against gripes against Indian cricket, which is not a bad starting point for an ill-tempered essay. It needs more patience than it is moral to possess to accept with equanimity the boringly relentless charge, made by overseas critics, that if India's any good, it is only so at home. What about the unofficial world champions then? They lost the one-off tie against India in 1996; the series against India in 1998; the series against Sri Lanka in 1999; and the Indian series again in 2001. Why is it mean and crafty and dishonourable for India to win in India but not for Australia to win in Australia; and likewise spavined and incompetent for India

---

* These pieces are selections from a small diary of personal gripes maintained by the author during 2001–02. The last of the pieces, 'Bad Language', was published as 'Bad Language: Post-Modern Bull...' in *The Vocabula Review*, 11(12), 18 December 2009.

to lose in Australia but not for Australia to lose in India? If you do not already know, the reason is that Indian pitches are doctored: they are 'mud tracks'—'treacherous' and 'two-faced'. Australian and English pitches are 'hard', 'true' and 'sporting'. Further, the weather is hot and humid and sweaty in the subcontinent ('typical stinking bloody hot day', as a placard from the Australian support group's enclosure proclaimed during the 2001 Test series), and specifically tailored to sap the energy of the Anglo-Saxon whose heroism, admirable as it is, is yet no compensation for the loss of body salts. (If Indian players, however, cannot cope with the sticky wickets of England on mornings when two blazers are inadequate to keep you from shivering and the ball stings your hands like dammit, then that is a case of straightforward cissiness). It is not just crumbling tracks and a turning ball the visitors have to deal with, it is also their crumbling and turning intestines, subjected as these are to excess gastric motility by dirty water and spiced curries. Plus, the umpires in the subcontinent are all bloody cheats: how can you expect to get through an entire Test series without allowing the ball to hit the pad except in every other over when you draw the neutral umpire? And worst of all, the morale of the visiting team is constantly placed in jeopardy when innocent team members are wantonly lured into match-fixing deals by sleazy subcontinental bookies. Not to mention subcontinental players who, when they are not engaged in bogus appealing, are tampering with the ball. And, lest we forget, the crowds: noisy, partisan, and incapable of seeing it is only a game. Now this is oriental discourse with a vengeance. The only reason I do not offer the theme, gratis, to a researcher in any Cultural Anthropology Department is the suspicion that seven or eight Ph.D. dissertations have probably already been written around it. (*Addendum*: All this was written before the Mike Denness affair. That's more grist to my mill and deserves a full-sized gripe all to itself. Watch, as they say, this space.)

*

Not that there isn't something in all this whining-disguised-as-analysis. But it is for us to criticize ourselves, isn't it? And there is something to be said for faults on both sides, isn't there? Now that that's been dealt with, and the subject of culpability raised, it's natural to turn on the Indian selectors. They dropped Srinath in the home series against England in 1993, since he had done so well in the immediately preceding Indian tour of South Africa. They rewarded Laxman for his 167 at Sydney by dropping him against the touring South Africans in 2000. They must not forget to dish out similar treatment to him again, lest his performance in the three Test series against Australia should go to his head (especially seeing that he had the temerity not to repeat that performance in South Africa). Ramesh has already got the axe. The selectors should persist with trying Dravid in the opening slot and screw up his career (apart from Ramesh's), the way they did, all those years ago, with that fine player Ashok Mankad. And the BCCI should do everything in its power to hang Wright for his Wrongs.

*

It must be said of most Indian experts on TV that they are some-times intolerable and at all other times deserve to be shot. It does not do your inner harmony any good when you are subjected—in a fakey dramatic whisper, at that—to some such item of profundity as: 'I'll tell you what, Tony. This is a crucial period of play. It's important for the Indians to put up as many runs as possible on the board. And the opposition, for their part, should aim for a few quick wickets.'

*

The most disgusting thing about watching cricket on TV is the wretched commercial ads at the end of every over—at least two, sometimes three, even four ads in a row, and repeated over after over. This is a plainly indecent and degrading spectacle. To begin with, can one think of anything more vulgar than two American junk-drink companies actually sponsoring cricket? (We are, let us remind ourselves, talking of a game which has inspired a mathema-tician like Hardy and a poet like Francis Thompson. Not to men-tion splendid people like you and me.) Our players are required to do idiotic and undignified things in the ads; and one presumes the money they receive must be good, for them to do these idiotic and undignified things—a fact that only makes the whole thing worse, if that is conceivable. One likes to see the players ambling between overs. One does not like to see advertisements for soft drinks or underwear or toothpaste. It is extremely trying, after each of two quick Indian wickets have fallen, to have to suffer some overweight, smug, self-satisfied child tell its doting parents why they must always remember to do the right thing by their moppet's dental hygiene by promoting the sales figure of Brand X Tooth-paste. I should be pleased to visit violent corporal punishment on such a child, and in so admitting I am confident that I am speak-ing for all non-hypocrites. Cuteness and cricket do not mix. This, among other reasons, is why this essay is not part of a collection titled *A Kurmudgeon's Komplaints*.

June 2001

Indian Institutions of Higher Learning

It is an old theme that institutions in India are gripped with a death wish. It is tragic that old themes like these have not yielded place to new facts. Institutional moribundity, as a feature of contemporary Indian society, continues to—so to speak—remain alive and kick-ing. We all have our own little explanations of this phenomenon, curmudgeons not exempted. It cannot hurt to unship a few gripes on the subject. (If it did hurt, some good might be expected to come out of it, but that, without a doubt, is too much to hope for.)

*

There are institutions and institutions: parliament, the press, the judiciary, and Indian Railways …One cannot take them all on board, even on the best of curmudgeonly days. I shall restrict myself, in very general terms, to educational and research institu-tions devoted to the cause of higher learning: in short, institutions of the type that one must expect to be exempt from the sort of criticism which the intellectuals governing and working in them think nothing of dishing out to other institutions such as parliament, the press, the judiciary, and Indian Railways ...

*

The worst type of institution of learning is the better type. It is the sort of institution that shines only by contrast. Shining is not difficult when one is functioning in an abyss. If you have steered clear of those boundless excesses of corruption, nepotism and incompetence which characterize the conduct of a majority of Indian institutions, you are in business. An institution such as this, which has not quite plumbed the depths of venality, begins to acquire a wholly bloated reputation for goodness. Relative excellence—in levels of vision or integrity or competence—is entirely compatible with absolute mediocrity. A matter for both sorrow and anger is that some of these institutions have actually had their genesis in genuinely admirable acts of creation and sustenance, presided over by institution builders of the highest calibre of intellect and dedication. An initially deserved reputation regrettably tends to be sustained over time for the simple reason that the distance between the institution and its environment continues to be maintained in its favour by a rate of descent into mediocrity for the institution which is less precipitous than that for the environment within which it operates. Worst of all, the institution begins to take its ill-deserved reputation seriously. Lack of commitment, slothfulness, back-stabbing, implicit intra-institutional social contracts for muted or non-existent internal criticism, absence of planning, a cynical disregard for work schedules—all of these vices are painlessly absorbed in the afflatus produced by an extravagant self-image (which has the advantage of public endorsement) that sits cosily with an attitude of moral righteousness and intellectual arrogance. Only, that is not the way the attitude comes across: in what can only be described as a brilliant inversion of the truth, the attitude on public display is one of uniform humility and kindness—the intellectual equivalent of the lord and master of the village engaging in feeding the poor. Tolerance of mediocrity is self-consciously advanced as the virtue of the genuinely good and great. This is a splendidly convenient arrangement in a context wherein nobody is going to nail the lie, to identify the 'kindness' for what it is, namely the tolerance, as John le Carre has said somewhere, that comes from no longer caring.

*

Many of the institutions of the type I have described above are ones which are badly strapped for resources. You'd think they would strive to conserve and enhance their resource base. They do neither. Attracting funding without selling out is admittedly not an easy task. It is also an impossible task when the institution's governing board, as is very often the case, is constituted by a set of grey eminences who have a vision that seldom extends beyond the lunch that will be served after the mandatory annual 2-hour meeting of the board, little of the commitment that is needed to discharge their obligations to the institution, and nothing at all of the willingness to remit office in favour of somebody younger and more productive. As for conserving resources, the profligacy with which these are consumed is often shocking. When anyone is moved at all to defend such practices, what is placed on offer is a certain spectacular high-mindedness that is above such petty considerations as assets, liabilities and cash flows. It is worth adding that some at least of these institutions have large numbers of economists on their faculty.

*

If the above is a model of cynical leadership, it is equally a model of cynical followership. Why rock the boat, when there is so much to be said for the prudential virtues of security of tenure, a reasonable wage, low marginal productivity, and a share in the internal distribution of power? As James Agee has said: 'the weak in courage are strong in cunning.' Even curmudgeons are occasionally moved to smile when they note that quite a few of these institutions have a large 'radical' element in them. These are dignified, gentlemanly radicals who make the supreme sacrifice of tolerating institutionally sub-optimal practices simply in order to have some sort of

anchoring while they are engaged in the self-denying task of serving the Larger Cause .... Since they are so utterly unencumbered
by any sense of irony, and so thoroughly cocooned in the insular
trappings of their own imagined virtue, they probably do not see
what excellent support they provide for the micro-foundations of
the neoclassical economics they so heartily despise: micro-foundations that were pithily summarized by the economist Frank Hahn
in the twin notions of 'private greed' and 'private rationality'.

*

To speak ill of Indian institutions, as I have done, is admittedly the
sort of churlish and ill-tempered violation of decent taste which
justly merits the stricture of 'curmudgeonliness;' above all else,
it is a flagrant affront to the dignity of that time-honoured Latin
injunction:

>   *de mortuis nil nisi bonum.*

August 2001

Teaching Them Young

Where the facility of a school exists, it is often of the most rudimen-
tary type—wanting in classrooms, desks, blackboards, and chalk.
And teachers. The phenomenon of school-less-ness is intimately
tied to that of child labour, which more often than not manifests
itself in a form—that of arduous unpaid domestic work—which is
routinely neglected by state and society alike. Such school education, as is provided, is geared to a system of certification in which
predictable and identifiable castes and socioeconomic groups are
enabled to press home the advantages of the accident of birth, while
others are simply left to their own devices. This appealing set of circumstances is nicely complemented by the recent move to rewrite
textbooks in such a way as to promote national pride through
orchestrated lying. The subject of the following diatribe has to do
with an aspect of elementary education, namely the extent, content
and nature of what school kids are required to learn, which would

be a major scandal were it not for the fact that, in this country, any concern over a phenomenon, however awful, is swiftly deflected by concern over a related phenomenon which is even more awful. But I am going to press on ahead regardless, without allowing the relentless worse to rescue the avoidable bad.

*

The present set of discontented mutters is inspired by the fact of having been found out in my strenuous but eventually unsuccessful attempt at indefinitely dodging the parental responsibility of sharing in the effort of passing my daughter's Grade III examination. On being challenged and made to render account, I have had to submit—with very poor grace, I have been told, just to rub it in—to the requirement of a more equitable distribution of the domestic misery entailed in imparting instruction to one's offspring. My daughter is seven-and-a-half years old, and her parents are a couple of broken reeds. Early qualms over her insistence, on the basis of her mentors' authority, that it was fine for her to talk of 'taddy beers' and 'tuth dekkay', have paled into insignificance in the light of the impossible muck the poor child is expected to learn by rote and reproduce, at copious length, in her exam papers. Allowing for some natural embarrassment over the language employed, it is instructive to recall what Maria Montessori said: 'Ah, before such dense and willful disregard of the life which is growing within these children, we should hide our heads in shame and cover our guilty faces with our hands!' (I respect the sentiment, though I should have put it a little differently myself, preferring as I do the style favoured by Phantom comics, which is something of the following order: '~@@#$***%$^&#'.) Here is a sample of the sort of stuff that is supposed to mould my daughter's mind:

'They were short and dark-skinned. The Dravidians had flat and short noses and thick lips.'
'Goddess Parvati in the form of peacock, is shown worshipping Siva, in the form of Lingam.'
'Increase of food production is known as Green Revolution. Our Government has taken a number of steps to increase the

agricultural production. Let us now list these steps' (followed by six numbered points demanding to be memorized).

'Write the abbreviation for each of the following:

Border Security Force, World Health Organization, Hindustan Machine Tools, Central Bureau of Investigation, United Arab Emirates, Param Vir Chakra.'

'A preposition is a word placed before a noun (or a pronoun) to show the relation in which the person or thing denoted by the noun stands to something else.'

'Words which *say* something are called verbs. All *saying*-words are verbs.'

'Any person can become a member of the co-operative society by giving a small amount. The members can have a share of profit. A co-operative society lends money to its members. The society charges only a very low rate of interest. The members can repay the money in easy installments.'

'Preservation and conservation of soil: Soil can be protected, preserved and conserved in the following ways:

1. Prevention of soil erosion by water, wind and rain: ...
2. Proper use of grasslands: ...
3. Prevention of cutting down trees: ...
4. Use of alternate materials in place of fertile soil: ...
5. Cultivation of crops in rotation: ...
6. Increasing the fertility of soil: ... '

'Some of these vegetables such as potato, onion, etc. are exported to countries all over the world. India earns valuable foreign exchange through these exports.'

'Quinine used in the treatment of malaria is obtained from the bark of the cinchona tree. Thulasi has an antiviral factor. ... Many antibiotics are also obtained from bacteria and fungi.'

One has to ask oneself what combination of lack of education, idiocy, and sadism informs the evil spirit of this country's educators that they should wish anything like the above on seven and eight year olds.

*

My childhood is one that has little in common with Laurie Lee's: there is no Cider with Rosie sort of thing to dwell lovingly on. Furthermore, curmudgeons are not moved to sentimental recollections of their youth. Even so, honesty compels me to admit, with proper shame over such mushiness, that it is with a distinctly nostalgic lump in the throat that I look back to my own childhood and the terrible education I received.

February 2002

Bad Language

*

George Orwell, in an essay titled 'Politics and the English Language', presented a brilliant example of how the beauty and clarity of words can, with a bit of determined effort, be metamorphosed into ugly, dense obfuscation. He translated, with devastating effect, a passage from Ecclesiastes into modern 'politicalese'. The result is a marvel of truth-telling through parody. Orwell's thesis of the willful destruction of good language and its transformation into gobbledygook remains valid for our own times, although it must be remarked that the agents of destruction have now changed. In today's world, it would be hardly fair to designate a politician as the principal villain of the piece. Blessed by illiteracy, he has little use for language, good or bad, preferring as he does to let his actions speak louder than mere words—actions that, more often than not, are of the type that land him in jail, whence he contests (and wins) elections. Orwell's politician's place has now been taken by the academic and s/he—take it from me—will require some dislodging from her/his seat of eminence.

*

It might be as well to slip in here the fact that I belong to the tribe of academics myself, but being only an economist, the charge of bad language does not stick to me nor, I may add (being a loyal sort of character), to my fellow practitioners. We economists, you see, take the greatest care to make ourselves very clearly understood, by stating everything in the form of unambiguously pellucid axioms, assumptions, definitions, remarks, lemmata, and theorems: our concern is always and only that others should have no difficulty in comprehending us, though we ourselves usually have a less than dim appreciation of what we say. The chief offenders I refer to are those that write in a language that is nominally English but is in reality a language called postmodern. Postmodern cuts across several disciplinary boundaries on its way to occupying its vast indisciplinary spaces. For long it was my belief that postmodern could only be written, not spoken, which, I thought, was why postmodern academics always cautiously read their papers at seminars, from beginning to end, without ever venturing to ad lib. But practice makes perfect, and if you catch them young, there is nothing you cannot teach them: these days, you will find children, fresh out of college, who speak the language fluently and extempore. And rudely, and with a personal edge. Such as to suggest that troglodytes like myself are incapable of spelling 'hermeneutics', are imprisoned in a 'Newtonian' view of the world, and are guilty of 'linear' thought. This is particularly hard to take, considering the facts (a) that my childhood triumphs in dictation were not always secured by cheating, (b) that I barely managed to pass my physics examination in school, and (c) that, from time to time, and in the cause of making a (modest) living, I am constrained to employ quadratic equations in my models.

*

Postmodernists are highly non-trivial persons who can be particularly severe on you if you express yourself badly as you would, for instance, by suggesting that you sometimes find it difficult to tell your left hand from your right, when what you really mean is that the negotiation of binary oppositions is a fraught event. With *that* kind of obtuse and low-brow mentality, how can people like you and me ever hope to come to any sort of grips with social theory, leave alone Social Theory? How can we aspire to arrive at any understanding of the world which is informed by a radical, democratic and fraternal sensibility, unless we choose to apprehend social reality in terms of the categories of aporia, hegemony, rupture, metanarrative, cyborg, resistance, *résistance, jouissance, différance, matérialité, localité,* embodied subjects, the subject as body, the body as subject, space, spaces, private spaces, public spaces? In what good cause of political intervention can we ever dare to engage if we have failed to interpret the world with that direct and humble lucidity which so thoroughly permeates a passage such as the following one—an excerpt from J. Derrida's *Dissemination,* translated by B. Johnson?

> You will ceaselessly be required to take this structural illusion into account. You should remark here only that that it does not arise as an aberrant error, an uncontrollable disorientation, or a capricious contingency of desire. On the contrary, it has to belong to a necessity inscribed *in situ,* within the overall organization and calculable functioning of the topography, so that the theater can finally succeed in being cruelly generalized, so that no nonplace whatsoever is left out of it, so that no pure origin (of creation, of the world, of the word, of experience, of all that is present in general) can stand guard over the stage as if derived from the intactness of some absolute opening. If that which, once it is framed, appears to be an element or an occurrence of opening is no longer anything but an aperture-effect that is topographically assignable, then nothing will indeed have taken place but the place.

How may I understand—leave alone transform—the world when I have not the resources of intellect and ability with which to understand the words with which to understand the world?

*

Arising from all of which, it gives me particular pleasure to offer the views of Sir Thomas Browne on the subject. I should explain that a tiny fragment of this great 17th century essayist's writing was recently unearthed by the Archival Section of the International Freemasonry of Curmudgeons (of which, if I may share a secret in confidence, I happen to be a member in good standing). The fragment will reveal that Browne, in addition to being a great physician and a great writer, was also a great prophesier, who foresaw

the blight of postmodern. I reproduce the fragment, for your benefit, with the special permission of the Brotherhood. Apart from
anything else, it affords me much jejune malice to give the p-m's a
taste of their own medicine.

SACRELIGIO ACADEMICI

(or)

HYPERGRAPHIA

By

Sir Thomas Browne

What cacophony of man exceedeth even the rabid howling of Cere-
brus in Hades is perdurably entrapt in the prose of Magister Johannes
Derrida: *litera scripta manet*. It belongeth to futurity, being *itself* futurity. Though it grow as old as Methuselah, it will ever be less than
youthfull, for it is *Poste-moderne*, which is the everlasting promise of
being, the contingency of imminence that defeateth the accomplish-
ment of becoming. But the Universe, which is governed not by
pseudo-paradox, repelleth the conceit of immortality that achieveth
its end by deluding the clock with the tricks of language: Poste-
moderne will have its moment, before it passeth into the oblivion
for which it was ordained. But while it lasteth, it will drive some
men to somnolent worship of its vainglorious claims, even as nepenthe dulleth the Faculties and induceth the sleep of insensate bliss. In
excess, and without the virtue of moderation, Poste-moderne, like
nepenthe, must cause men to succumb to that condition which Vir-
gil hath felicitously described as *rari nantes in gurgite vasto*. Whether
its Moment be a long one must depend on the span of time it taketh
a man to penetrate the deceiving armour of the king's new habili-
ments which, to one of vision, would hide not the breadth of a
fig's leaf. In truth, that abomination which is the language of Poste-
moderne sucketh the blood of wisdom and sappeth the Common
Sense of man by lixiviation. 'Tis the distillation of sapience to boldly
eschew the obliquity of denomination, so that bovine voidance is
apprehended by its meet and proper nomenclature, and receiveth
the appellation it deserveth, being only, and in perfect measure, that
which it is, which is bull

*

Here ends the fragment, with the (presumably) last word on the page partially obliterated by coffee stains caused, no doubt, by Sir Thomas' carelessness. 'Bovine voidance' is the same thing as 'bull'-what? Sadly, we shall never know. But I would like to suggest that a very plausible answer can be found if we are willing to make a shrewd, if hermeneutically coarse, guess. Needless to say, the guesswork is greatly aided by good, old-fashioned, Newtonian, linear extrapolation.

Reference

Derrida, Jacques.(1981), *Dissemination*, trans. Barbara Johnson. Chicago: University of Chicago Press.

15

Jai Ho, Jeeves!*

(An Advanced Sociological Analysis of Slumdog Millionaire)

Stop me if you have heard this before, but there is no smooth without a rough, as I have always maintained. Ask Bertram and he will tell you that there is no good in this world which is unqualified, if that is the word I want. Take the case of my man Jeeves. The fellow bursts with brains and loyalty, and his worth, to borrow one of his own favourite gags, is beyond the price of rubies. But grow a moustache, or wear purple socks, or tie a garish tie, and the blighter can be relied upon to cut up nasty. Under these circs, he will exhibit a moody, sullen, cold, and unfriendly side to his nature. Dashed unpleasant, I mean to say. Such as at this time I speak of now, just minutes before our departure for the airport, to catch our flight to the city of Mumbai, in order to get as far away as dictated by the demands of prudence (for reasons much too complex to enter into now) from Madeline Bassett and Sir Roderick Glossop and Honoria Glossop and Roderick Spode and my Aunt Agatha and a host of other prominent blots upon the Wooster landscape. As we waited for the taxi to bear us away to the airport, Jeeves busied himself with a pair of scissors, snipping

---

*The inspiration for this was supplied to the author by Shiva Shankar. The blame is mutual. (I may add that I had offered the essay for publication in a sociological journal to an editor-friend, who continues to be an editor.)

away at the baggage tags from a previous journey, and snipping, let me tell you, in a dashed marked manner.

'Jeeves', I said.
'Sir?'
'You snip away, let me tell you, in a dashed marked manner.'
'Indeed, sir?'
'And that eyebrow of yours, Jeeves.'
'Sir?'

'It quivers. Like the dickens. Why does your eyebrow quiver, Jeeves?'

'I am sorry if it occasions you distress, sir. But the quivering of my eyebrow is an involuntary action—one upon which I have no deliberate control—triggered by the sight of objects that may be described as especially loathsome and repulsive___'

'And what do you see about you, Jeeves, that is especially loathsome and repulsive?' (Bertram being suave, as you can see.)

'Forgive me sir, but those three yellow pieces of string you wear over your jacket like a cross-belt are not, if I may borrow a phrase from the poet John Keats, a thing of beauty—nor, indeed, a joy forever.'

'You refer, Jeeves, to my Sacred Thread, with which I have adorned myself, that I might gain an entrée into the world of India's most exclusive and elite society. It is my little bow in the direction of ethnic *chic*. You would not pronounce it soigné, Jeeves?'

'It is, conceivably, soigné, sir, for a *brahmacharyya* to sport his *yajno pavitra* on his bare torso upon his ordination as a *dwija* on the occasion of his *upanayanam* ceremony, but in your own case, if I may be permitted___'

'Jeeves!'
'Sir?'
'What drivel is this?'
'Not drivel, sir: Sanskrit.'
'I can do without the Sanskrit, Jeeves.'
'Very well, sir.'
'Put a sock in the Sanskrit, Jeeves.'
'Very well, sir.'

'I can take the Sanskrit or leave it, Jeeves, and right now I am dashed well inclined to leave it.'

'Just as you say, sir.'
'And now, to return to the *res*. Where were we?'
'We were in the middle of an exchange, sir, on an especially loathsome and repulsive object___'.

'There is no need to be personal, Jeeves. Enough. I have other things upon my mind. There will be no further talk of the sartorial, cultural or social appropriateness or otherwise of my Sacred Thread. I am preoccupied by matters of more immediate import. Not to put too fine a point on it, I am in a bit of a twitter. Indeed, and I state this with manly candour, I am all in a doo-dah. I need you, Jeeves, to rally around your young master in his hour of peril. I have just heard over the telephone that the British Council in Mumbai has arranged for me to turn up, upon our arrival there, at a television studio, to be interviewed for my opinion of the film *Slumdog Millionaire* which, as you are no doubt aware, has been nominated for the Nobel Prize.'

'A somewhat unlikely contingency, if I may say so, sir. The Nobel Committee does not award Prizes to moving pictures. It is possible that what you have in mind is the Oscar.'

'The Oscar, then, Jeeves. Let us not quibble. Quibbling, if that's what we're up to, is going to take us nowhere, in the light of the horror that is upon me. Do you realize I am going to be interviewed on television by the woman Barker Dutt?'

'Why, may I ask, sir, do you view the matter with such anxiety?'

'Why? Why? Have you any idea what kind of woman this Barker Dutt is? She is a ghastly female, Jeeves. Ghastlier far than Madeline Bassett and Honoria Glossop and my Aunt Agatha all rolled into one. She shakes her head and rolls her eyes and waves her arms and laughs like a hyena. She does all these things in a way calculated to inspire pity and terror in the subject. And then she puts words in your bally mouth, Jeeves. She's going to trip me up. She's going to unleash a lynch mob on me when all I want is to be able to look back on my travels and say that the natives were friendly and we decided to stay the night. She will lay traps for me, Jeeves. If I say I don't like the film, she'll accuse me of influencing the judges against handing out the Nobel Prize to the film. If I say I do like it, she'll accuse me of endorsing all the bad things the film says about India. She'll say, with no regard for my Sacred Thread, that I'm just spoiling their fun for them, depriving them of the small pleasures of lynching their untouchables and burning their women and fiddling while millions of people have to live in the poverty and squalor of their slums. I'm dashed if I do, and I'm dashed if I don't. I'm caught on the horns of that thing—what d'you call it, Jeeves?—that thing on the horns of which people do get caught from time to time.'

'A dilemma, sir?'

'A di-by-golly-lemma is precisely the thing on the horns of which I find myself caught. What will I do, Jeeves?'

'You may wish to consider a stratagem which combines the measures of Stout Denial and Wearing Your Opponent Down with Non-Sequiturs, sir. I would advance, if I may, the virtue of not ever answering Miss Barker Dutt's questions. Instead, I would advocate your adopting the simple and charming expedient of responding to her every query by breaking out into song. I am inclined to suggest just two words of a popular ditty from the picture, executed to this tune: "Jai Ho"!'

'"Jai Ho", Jeeves?'
'That was very well done, sir, if I may say so.'
'Shall I try again? Jai Ho? How does that sound, eh? Jai Ho!'
'Excellent, sir.'

'Well, there's no denying it, Jeeves. Your plan will, in all likelihood, extricate the young master from the old hole. I may yet expect to get away with my life from the Barker Menace in Mumbai. I suppose I owe you a debt of gratitude. Since you feel so strongly about it, I'll make the supreme sacrifice, and eschew the joys of the Sacred Thread. "Eschews" it is, is it not Jeeves?'

'You employ what M. Flaubert always called the *mot juste*, sir. But there really is no need for you to take the trouble of removing the Thread from your person. I regret to say, sir, that I have accidentally severed the Thread with my scissors, and detached it from its moorings.'

'Accidentally, did you say, Jeeves?'
'It was a most regrettably inadvertent act upon my part, sir.'
'Really, Jeeves?'
'Without a peradventure of a doubt, sir.'
'Jai Ho, Jeeves.'
'Very good, sir.'

16

Language and Representation or, More Modestly, Mathematical Economics and Poverty*

Since economists are equal to anything, and economics is largely a matter of what (and how) economists write, economics, in practice, could be virtually anything you cared to specify. To introduce a measure of sanity into proceedings, the field has here been narrowed down to one sample of what economists can get up to when they are purportedly studying the phenomenon of poverty. This sample covers the case of what one might, in a desperate bid for comprehensiveness, allude to as analytico-positivistic-moral-philosophico-mathematical economics—work that is intensive in the squiggles of symbolic logic; 'impossibilities'; tricky variational arguments, and *de rigueur* references to Marx and Engels to guard against the charge of fiddling while Rome burns.

While the mathematical whizz-kids look down their splendid noses on their less favoured brethren, not least the data-grubbers among them, the latter tend to give themselves airs of moral superiority: they may not sparkle, but at least they do relevant and socially responsible work, which is what keeps them honest (and

* This essay was originally published, under the same title, in *Vocabula Review*, 12(11), November 2010.

poor). The sad fact is that both types of economist are equally despised by that variety of radical scholar—now increasingly visible on the horizon—that thinks nothing of shooting off tracts with titles like 'Discursive Displacement of the Subject in Poverty: The Ideological Complicity of "*Homo Oeconomicus*"', or '*de la pauvrete*: Gendered Subjectivity and Patriarchal Reification in Statistical Re-presentation and the Production of an Official Discourse on Deprivation', destined for publication in *The Post-Structuralist Critical Review*, and not in some low-brow 1,500 words-an-article journal like *Math Econ Letters* or—unmentionably worse—*Applied Journal of Compulsory Regression Research*.

The sample that follows should serve to underline the basis for the sort of warning that D.B. Wyndham-Lewis (the first 'Beachcomber') might have issued, had he been around, to complacent math-econ practitioners: 'Watch out, you cads! The post-mods are just round the corner!'

*

Measuring Poverty Vaguely

Poverty, it will be argued here, is most sensibly comprehended as a *vague* object. (For a completely unrelated view of a totally different problem, the reader is referred to the illuminating and otherwise interesting paper by Starsky and Hutch (1982): 'Consequentialist Choice on a Deontic Topological Space with a Continuum of Preferences: A Real-valued Representation of Wrawls in the Light of Nosick', *Zeitschrift fur Praktischen Logisches Denken und Scharf Armut (Journal of Practical Reasoning and Acute Poverty*), Vol. 2, No. 2, 28–38. Motivationally, this notion draws heavily on the view that both utilitarianism and prioritarianism fall outside the purview of what may be called *objectively rationalizable rational objectivity* (see the Special Issues on 'Poverty, Analysis, and Measurement' in *Proceedings of the Socratic Society*, Athens, 1992; 'Analysis, Poverty, and Measurement', *Bjro Strindberg Distinguished Lectures on the Ethical Dimension of Humanistic Fuzzy Subsets*, Reykjavic, 1996; and

'Measurement, Poverty, and Analysis', *Archivis di Fibonacci-Marx Instituzione*, Arezzo, 2003). The problem, as will be readily apparent, is rendered mathematically tractable when certain fundamental results in measure theory are exploited. (On exploitation, in more general spaces, see Marx; also Engels; and most of all, Marx-Engels.)

Letting $\mathbb{R}_+$ and $\mathbb{R}_{++}$ stand for the non-negative real line and the positive real line, respectively, consider the class of fuzzy poverty functions M, given by

$$M \equiv \{m: \mathbb{R}_+ \to [0,1] \mid m(0) = 1; \exists z \in \mathbb{R}_{++} : m\downarrow \text{ on } [0,1]; \lim_{s \to z} m(s) = 0; \& m(s) = 0 \forall s > z\}.$$ (m is assumed to be at least 2-C differentiable.) Define the *fuzzy headcount ratio* H as $H \equiv (1/n(\mathbf{x}))\sum_i m(x_i ; \mathbf{x})$, where $n(\mathbf{x})$ is the dimensionality of $\mathbf{x}$.

The following result is true.

Theorem. There exists no $m \in M$ such that H simultaneously satisfies strong monotonicity, weak scale invariance, strict replication invariance, semi-strict translation invariance, quasi-proper sub-group consistency, almost-decomposability, wobbly symmetry, and doubtful upward transfer.

Proof. Straightforward. ([The proof is available, on request, with the author (viz. myself). Errors, if any, will be stoutly defended and otherwise firmly and sarcastically dealt with in my 'Rejoinder' (forthcoming), which will also carry an appendix relating to 'Poverty on Sets of Measure Zero'.])

Remark. The requirement that m be differentiable can be relaxed without much damage to our result: these, and related variational problems, have been completely and elegantly characterized in four of my forthcoming papers: 'Poverty Without Differentiability', 'Poverty Without Integrability', 'Poverty Without Integrity' and 'Poverty Without Poverty'.

*

Poverty, anyone?

17

Writing Economics in Exactly 300 Words: Two Samples in the Tradition of J.B. Morton ('Beachcomber')*

Explanation

*W*hen the Editors of Eostre did me the signal honour of inviting a contribution from me, I found myself torn between being flattered by the invitation and being unprepared for it. It was wonderful to be asked at all, but less than inspiriting to be asked at a time when various unmet deadlines were snapping at my heels, and papers presided over by nasty editors were displaying a tendency to contain neat theorems which I hadn't yet succeeded in proving. I am due to retire in a year's time, and—overcome with self-pity—I decided I wouldn't, in the twilight of my career, kill myself attempting to write another grim-death, serious paper in the midst of all the sorrows of the uncompleted papers I was wading through. Hence this article.

I should explain that J.B. Morton (1893–1979), who practiced his craft under the pseudonym of 'Beachcomber', wrote a column—from 1924

---

*This essay was originally published as: 'How To Write Economics in Exactly Three Hundred Words in the Tradition of J.B. Morton (Beachcomber)' (2013): *Eostre*.

to 1975—titled 'By the Way' for (to put it mildly) a less-than-radical English newspaper The Daily Express. Morton's own views were also often reactionary, but inspired by a genius for lunacy which those who have read him will agree is very hard to resist. I decided, in a fit of self-indulgence, to do a J.B. Morton on Economics: his occasional tiny pieces on the subject (with captions such as 'The Money Market', 'Financial Note', etc.) were marvels of plausible and wholly nonsensical gobbledygook which captured the nuances of the argot, without the slightest regard for sanity, in hilarious parody. And so I resolved that, for once, I would abjure the stuffed shirt and treat my subject with a little less deference than it is customary to accord it.

It remains to add that it would be unquestionably disingenuous on my part to deny that the first of the ensuing two pieces has been inspired at least a little by malice: I hope it will prove possible for the reader to condone this. This is not an unreasonable expectation, if one allows for the fact that we are all political creatures and that economics is less like physics—and less than entirely the monopoly of Walmart—than we are given to pretending it is. The second piece is a tribute to the hordes of frighteningly high-brow and well-read infant-prodigy-mathematical-economists that are being turned out in the contemporary world of economics scholarship, and it emanates from the sober realization that I have somehow blundered through a career as an Indian economist with very scant knowledge of two of its essential components: Differential Topology and Bengali. Just in case there is any doubt on this score, the reader has my word for it that the piece is inspired entirely by affection and admiration—and some wholly good-natured ribbing. After all, in the course of a visit to the Delhi School in 1984 I once heard one of your most distinguished members, Professor Kaushik Basu, sing. (In a loose manner of speaking.) My case rests.

*

Buy the Way: A Column on Mainly Econo and Some Other Mystic Propositions

by

Toothcomber

(Toothcomber is an intellectual heir of Beachcomber. He is protected by international copyright law, or a thick hide, or something on that order.)

Growing at 10 Per Cent

The key to the problem is raising the right question. For—we have this on the authority of Maynard Keynes, and if we don't we can confidently rely on the reader to be ignorant of the fact—how can you get novel, intelligent, relevant answers if you don't ask novel, intelligent, relevant questions? There is only one such question to be asked about the Indian economy. Can we sustain a 10 per cent rate of growth? It helps, in answering the question, to be an expert who descends on India from Mount Olympus every now and then in order to advise the unwashed millions on the virtues of FDI in multi-brand retail. This is the kind of experience that enables you to relate the answer to the state of the economy's fundamentals. The answer being that a 10 per cent rate of growth is eminently feasible provided the fundamentals are behaving as they should. That is to say, all we require are the correct market sentiments, investor confidence, uninterrupted FII activity, (de)regulatory frameworks in place, moving the reform process forward, forex reserves, belief in WTO, tax buoyancy, fiscal discipline, selective privatization, discriminating privatization, indiscriminate privatization, one dream budget a year, a sober view of expenditure on capital formation, civilized (i.e., low) levels of social sector spending, targeted anti-poverty programmes (increasingly programs), partial convertibility on the capital account, full convertibility on the capital account, sound corporate governance, keeping M3 on target, ditto M4, M5, M6, M7, M8 and M9, flexible labour laws, a level playing field, India Shining, India Rising, and smart talk ('at this point in time'; 'major players'; 'bottomline'; 'at the end of the day'; 'India will have to take a call on this'; 'this is my take on the subject'; 'the NIFTY graph says it all').

The Price of Onions

Professor xxx-xxxxx xxxxxxx-xxxxxxxxxxx is eminently qualified to be one of India's greatest economists, possessing, as he does, a name that is doubly double-barrelled, and the distinction of having mastered Apostol's *Real Analysis* by his third birthday, not to mention that of reciting, at age five, all of the Great Poet's verse *backward*, in addition to a somewhat distressing disposition to break out, without warning, into snatches of semi-classical music, listening to which—truth to tell—can be a fate worse than death. Addressing a press conference, he complimented, as was his democratic and inclusive wont, the reporter's acumen in unleashing the labyrinthine ramifications associated with his foundationally complex question on the sudden spurt in the price of onions. Denying any deontological justification for the phenomenon, he however invited speculation on a possibly consequentialist rationalization for having to pay more for the earthy, sturdy, modest, self-effacing and profoundly unoffending vegetable. Drawing on Tolstoy and Marx, Professor xxxxxxx-xxxxxxxxxx suggested that a properly adequate answer to the question would probably entail a close analogy with the quest for a proof of Riemann's Hypothesis. He drew the press corps' attention to his recently published paper on 'Poverty on Sets of Measure Zero', as also to his forthcoming address to the International Association of Fuzzy Ethicists, to be held in Zurich, on 'Transfinite Demand for a Perishable Commodity with Vague Preferences on a Rawls–Nozick–Chebychev Continuum of Non-Negative Reals', which, the reporter who had set it all off was assured, to his (the reporter's) eternal gratification, he had, in fact, partially anticipated with his brilliant question. At the end of the meeting, the assembled reporters climbed up on their chairs and gave the Professor a thunderous ovation, before getting down to the business of addressing, in earnest, the *pyaaj pakoris* at the ensuing high tea.

About the Author

S. Subramanian is Former Professor, Madras Institute of Development Studies (MIDS). He has been awarded a post-retirement, two-year National Fellowship by the Indian Council of Social Science Research (ICSSR). An elected Fellow of the Human Development and Capability Association (HDCA), Subramanian has worked extensively on measurement and other aspects of poverty, inequality, and demography, and on topics in collective choice theory, welfare economics and development economics. His work has been published in journals such as *Journal of Development Economics*, *Economics and Philosophy*, *Social Choice and Welfare*, and *Theory and Decision*. He is the recipient (along with his co-author) of the 2001 Dudley Seers Memorial Prize awarded to the best article published in the *Journal of Development Studies*.

An established scholar in poverty and inequality, he has edited/authored the following titles:

- *Themes in Development Economics: Essays in Honour of Malcolm Adiseshiah*, New Delhi.
- *Measurement of Inequality and Poverty* (Readers in Economics Series), New Delhi. *Illfare in India: Essays on India's Social Sector in Honour of S. Guhan* (with Barbara Harriss-White), Delhi: SAGE Publications, 1999.
- *India's Development Experience: Selected Writings of S. Guhan*, New Delhi. *Rights, Deprivation, and Disparity: Essays in Concepts and Measurement* (Collected Essays Series), New Delhi.
- *Poverty, Inequality, and Population: Essays in Development and Applied Measurement* (with D. Jayaraj), New Delhi. (paperback edition: 2012).
- *The Poverty Line* (Oxford India Short Introductions Series), New Delhi.